NEED TO KNOW

HOW TO ARM YOURSELF AND SURVIVE
ON THE HEALTHCARE BATTLEFIELD

NEED
TO
KNOW

DARWIN HALE

LIONCREST
PUBLISHING

NEED TO KNOW

How to Arm Yourself and Survive on the Healthcare Battlefield

ISBN   978-1-61961-837-4 *Hardcover*

978-1-61961-838-1 *Paperback*

978-1-61961-836-7 *Ebook*

CONTENTS

INTRODUCTION.................................... 9

PART I: THE BATTLEFIELD

1. WHAT IF I TOLD YOU THERE WAS A WAR? 31
2. CASUALTIES OF WAR 49
3. ANOTHER ENEMY: THE HEALTHCARE SYSTEM........... 69

PART II: FIGHTING THE GOOD FIGHT: ARMING YOURSELF

4. NUTRITION: YOU ARE WHAT YOU EAT.......................... 87
5. MOVEMENT: DON'T GUM UP THE WORKS 107
6. MINDSET: YOU CAN WORRY YOURSELF SICK 123

PART III: GETTING HEALTHCARE TO CARE FOR YOU

7. WHAT'S WORKING WELL RIGHT NOW........................ 145
8. TECHNOLOGY 163
9. HEALTHCARE MODEL FOR THE FUTURE.................... 185
10. STAKEHOLDERS WORKING TOGETHER PROMOTE EFFICIENCIES.. 199

CONCLUSION 221

ABOUT THE AUTHOR 235

INTRODUCTION

I am not an advocate for frequent changes in laws and constitutions, but laws and institutions must go hand in hand with the progress of the human mind. As that becomes more developed, more enlightened, as new discoveries are made, new truths discovered, and manners and opinions change, with the change of circumstances, institutions must advance also to keep pace with the times. We might as well require a man to wear still the coat which fitted him when a boy as civilized society to remain ever under the regimen of their barbarous ancestors.

—THOMAS JEFFERSON (1816)[1]

What if I told you there was a war costing the United States over 250,000[2] lives a year and trillions of dollars? The nation would be up in arms, there would be demonstra-

---

1   http://www.foundingfatherquotes.com/quote/908

2   http://www.bmj.com/company/wp-content/uploads/2016/05/medical-errors.pdf

tions everywhere, and the media would fill the airwaves with commentary.

Why do I ask? Because that is exactly what is happening in our country today. Most of us have no idea this is going on. We don't know who the enemy is. But the enemy is here, right under our noses, draining our resources, killing off our population, and then sending us the bill. The sad truth is that the enemy is our very own healthcare system.

Healthcare is a 3.3 trillion-dollar annual industry,[3] comprising almost 18 percent of the Gross Domestic Product (GDP).[4] Every year, over 250,000 people die from medical errors alone, but there are not enough people talking about it. Our healthcare system has failed to evolve alongside other industries, making it complicated, inadequate, and dangerous. Sooner or later it affects all of us. It will affect you. It will affect the people you love.

Whether you like it or not, you're headed into battle.

SURVIVING THE HEALTHCARE BATTLEFIELD

Here is the truth: at some point, every civilian in this

---

3   https://www.cms.gov/Research-Statistics-Data-and-Systems/Statistics-Trends-and-Reports/
     NationalHealthExpendData/downloads/highlights.pdf

4   https://www.cms.gov/Research-Statistics-Data-and-Systems/Statistics-Trends-and-Reports/
     NationalHealthExpendData/downloads/highlights.pdf

nation is going to be drafted onto the healthcare battlefield. Whether we are taking care of our parents or loved ones and making decisions on their behalf, or taking care of ourselves, we will all inevitably have to face a tour of duty and confront the enemy.

We don't have a choice in the matter, but we do have an obligation. We have an obligation to serve ourselves and others. As citizens, children, parents, and friends, we owe it to ourselves and to our country to be active participants in our own care. We will live better and drive trillions of dollars out of the system.

Citizens everywhere need to get involved in their own health: ask questions, do the research, and take matters into their own hands. Being an active participant in our own care is the opposite of how the system trains us to behave. We're trained to be passive, but we can't afford to be anymore.

Here's an example. I was at the doctor's office recently and shortly after she arrived, the nurse took my "vitals." She asked me to step on a scale, so she could determine my weight, but then she never let me touch the scale. She simply took the reading and noted it in my file. When she took my blood pressure, she didn't tell me the reading. I had to ask. She wasn't necessarily trying to withhold information; she was behaving in accordance with the system.

I couldn't rely on her to stand up to the enemy. It was up to me, as it is for all of us, to be active in my own health.

Most of us, unfortunately, put that control in the hands of others who are part of a system that puts us at risk. It's a system that hasn't evolved to meet the new and changing needs of the population. When I was the healthcare director for AT&T, I would travel the world presenting at conferences. One thing I would always ask my audience was, "What is the most important thing in your life?" Almost everyone said, "my health." Next, I would ask how many miles their vehicle got per gallon of gas, and they could easily tell me. Then I would ask them what percentage of return their 401(k) was yielding. They could easily rattle off their results. When I asked them what their HDL/LDL ratio was, all I would get were blank looks in response. Most people don't know what that metric is, even though they say their health is the most important thing to them. They knew more about their gas mileage or retirement than they did about their cholesterol ratio. That, to me, identified a gap, one I've been working on fixing ever since.

They were not prepared for battle. They were not armed with their most powerful ammunition: knowledge. Without the right information, there is no way to navigate the healthcare landscape or make correct, *informed* decisions. The decisions that need to be made regarding individual-

expensive on both a personal and a global scale. Medical bills are the number one cause of personal bankruptcy in the US[6]—and a lot of those people actually have insurance. The healthcare system should be improving lives. Instead, it's gobbling up retirements. It's destroying legacies that should be left to our children.

One of the challenges we face as citizens is that the way the healthcare system works is largely unknown. It is a vast and complex entity, yet it has the greatest doctors, caregivers, and technology in the world. People from around the globe travel to the US to receive medical care because our innovations and skills are unparalleled. Yet, at the same time, the rate of medical errors and some hospital readmission rates are very high. It is a system that can cure or kill you.

Out of the 2.6 million deaths in this country every year, 7 to 8 percent of them are from a medical error.[7] Imagine if that same percentage of defects were attributed to the airline, hospitality, or banking industry. There would be mass upheaval! The healthcare statistics are astronomical on both the positive and negatives sides, which is why it is so critical for people to understand where the good parts are and avoid the bad parts.

---

6   https://www.kff.org/report-section/
     medical-debt-among-people-with-health-insurance-consequences-of-medical-debt/

7   http://www.bmj.com/company/wp-content/uploads/2016/05/medical-errors.pdf

The prescription for survival on the healthcare battle-field is to be well armed and prepared. Eisenhower said, "Plans are worthless, but planning is everything."[8] By that, he meant the mental process of planning, preparing, and thinking things through is where you get the value. Intelligence, training, equipment, tactics, and strategies in the proper combination are essential for success. The military battlefield and the healthcare landscape are similar in this regard.

The casualties of war on the healthcare battlefield are caused by more than just chronic disease. Cancer and heart failure are known enemies, but medical errors and noncompliant behavior also lead to suffering and death.[9] Think about disease in the same way you think about a terrorist plotting an attack on your city, except in this case, the city is your body. It is imperative that you are able to simplify the complexity of the medical jargon and sift through the reports to pull out the pieces of information that matter to you. Make a battle plan that identifies your specific risks and protects you from them.

The best way to be armed for battle is to mitigate the risk by being knowledgeable about nutrition, movement, and mindset. Nutrition is probably the number one contrib-

8   Dwight D. Eisenhower, *Public Papers of the Presidents of the United States* (National Archives and Records Service, Government Printing Office, 1957), 818.

9   https://www.cdc.gov/nchs/fastats/leading-causes-of-death.htm

uting factor to overall health and wellness. Movement is necessary to get the blood flowing, strengthen the muscles, and distribute nutrients from one body part to another and flush out the toxins. The wrong mindset leads to stress and the very real condition of "worrying yourself sick."[10] The most effective armament of this war is understanding how wellness can be used to fight disease.

A DUAL PERSPECTIVE

As a young man, I worked in a nonpartisan position for Senator Bob Graham of Florida. One of my assignments was to research national healthcare policies. Later, that research led me to a job with IBM, where we worked on what eventually became the "cloud" we talk about today. I was doing research for IBM and later AT&T to build their healthcare business strategy. AT&T thought we could help our healthcare customers as they evolved in the industry. To this day, I remain thankful to the generous leaders of the Fortune 500 healthcare companies who helped me to understand the industry. As one executive put it, "I really hope you are successful in what you want to do but I want to warn you—the healthcare roadside is littered with skeletons." Eventually, I went on to the executive ranks to lead a part of the AT&T business, serving our Fortune 500 healthcare customers.

---

10   Walter Bradford Cannon, *Bodily Changes in Pain, Hunger, Fear, and Rage* (New York: Appleton-Century-Crofts, 1929).

Before I gained that insight, I joined the Army. At seventeen, just three weeks after I graduated from high school, I left for basic training at Fort Knox, a first step in a journey that eventually led me to becoming a military officer and serving in operations all over the world. One of the most valuable aspects of my education was learning about the evolution of the military and, in particular, its decision-making process. As a military police officer, I often read the words on the organization's crest: "Assist, Protect, Defend." Later, when I was working with the Special Forces community, the motto "Free the oppressed" rang true.

These have stayed with me over the years. They are not just catchphrases; they have become constant themes throughout my life. They are now at the core of what I'm fighting for in the healthcare industry.

Since its inception, the military has been interested in what skills commanders need to win battles, and who wins wars and why. They study war strategy as a science and constantly make improvements, test analytics, and shift tactics. The military determined, after hundreds of years of research, that one of the key elements of a winning strategy is accurate and swift decision making. In a scenario where two armies of equal skill have the same equipment, the army that is better able to make decisions in the midst of action will win.

As an officer, I went through rigorous training on the Military Decision-Making Process (MDMP). The first step is called *mission analysis* and requires that an individual be able to process several types of information at once: What are the likely enemy avenues of approach? How many roads are there into the site? How many fields? How dense are the woods surrounding it? Are there any rivers and how are they impacted by the seasons? The ability to know what kinds of questions to ask, understand the answers, and weigh them all against each other is vital to success. This has always stuck with me. When I was the healthcare director for AT&T and had problems to solve, I would look not just at my mission, but go two levels up in the chain of command to understand the larger missions I was supporting, allowing that to drive my decision making and unify the greater effort.

After 9/11, those in the military discovered that terrorists exhibit many of the same behaviors and patterns as criminals. Increasingly, terrorism-afflicted sites were treated like crime scenes, through the use of DNA analysis, fingerprints, and other forensics. There was a fusion between the military police and the special operations community, which I was privileged enough to work in for seven life-changing years.

The United States Special Operations Command (USSO-COM) has an exclusive program designed to ensure its headquarters personnel have relevant skills to support the people on the frontlines. Because of my diverse background, I applied and was selected for the program. Subsequently, I was trained and deployed to work as part of an elite Special Operations Forces (SOF) team. I worked alongside the best of the best. My developmental path in life was sealed through the experience, and it instilled in me a deep understanding of how a unified effort can conquer a life-threatening situation.

After many years with Special Operations, I returned to the conventional forces and ultimately became a colonel. I was deputy commander of a 15,000-member organization and chief of detectives of the Criminal Investigative Division (CID). Think of the television show *NCIS*, just the Army Reserve version. The really interesting thing about this group is that in their civilian jobs they worked for the FBI, DEA, SWAT, Border Patrol, and other elite law-enforcement organizations. We were able to take the best of each organization and combine them in our uniformed fight against terrorism.

Thirteen years ago, I left corporate America and my civilian career as the health director at AT&T to start my own business, Advocate Health Advisors. It was a decision largely fueled by my mother, specifically her health. When she turned sixty-five, I saw her struggle with all of the complicated decisions surrounding Medicare. She asked for my help to figure it out, which even I struggled to do. Even as a well-educated and accomplished person—a lieutenant colonel in the army and a corporate executive with an MBA—I could not make sense of the system. I called a trusted friend from the military, who was now in the insurance business. He gave me the advice and counsel I needed to get my mom set up properly.

The experience triggered my interest in the healthcare challenges facing the senior population. If my mom and I found it this hard, surely there must be others who needed help too. From my background conducting research for the Florida senator and later at IBM, I knew that 5 percent of patients are responsible for 50 percent of the healthcare spending.[11] A good portion of that 5 percent is composed of the senior population, which is growing rapidly, and will continue to do so for a long time.

I put my unique set of skills to work and identified waste throughout the healthcare process. I knew from experience that change was possible, but that it would have to be fought for. I also knew what it looked like when it worked. The evolution of the military and the lessons it had learned throughout the years was a strong example of how a behemoth organization, much like the healthcare industry itself, was capable of making wide-scale, sweeping change to increase efficiency and effectiveness.

---

11   https://meps.ahrq.gov/data_files/publications/st354/stat354.shtml

I dug in further and discovered that the healthcare system is fragmented, whereas other industries are integrated. Some industries are customer-driven, but somehow in healthcare, when our very lives are on the line, this isn't the case. Consumers do not have the luxury of shopping around for the best value. The system is divided across specialists and departments, most of which don't communicate with each other.

We are at a point of convergence in technology. There are many emerging innovations that are coming to market at an unprecedented rate, all of which will improve the healthcare experience and change the way we live. Processing power, reduced microchip costs, the mapping of the genome, electronic medical records, and countless other cutting-edge discoveries make this an exciting time. One problem, however, is that we are already far behind in the knowledge we should have of the healthcare system. The future of healthcare and technology is surging forward, and patients need to be educated on their new options. It is a case of irresistible force meeting an immovable object.

As Toby Cosgrove, the former CEO of the Cleveland Clinic, said, "healthcare is a team sport." We need to know who else is on the team, who's fighting the enemy along with us. Our allies are all around us, and yet most of us have no idea who they are.

WHY THIS BOOK?

Long before I heard the motto of the special forces, I had a strong calling to free the oppressed. Initially, this manifested in helping other kids who were bullied at school. I'm not a big person in stature, and never have been, but it has always bothered me when bigger kids pick on smaller kids. I learned then that you must stick up for yourself and others. This carried over when I entered the army, joined the military police, and eventually worked my way up the ranks to become colonel. I've seen oppression and horror throughout the world, and I have always been on the side of protecting those who are under attack.

When I retired from the military a few years ago, I still felt the need to serve. Even though my uniformed service is over, my service to the nation and to the oppressed will continue as long as I am alive. It continues through my company and the people we are able to educate and help. I've been able to retool Advocate Health Advisors to perform at a higher level and become more community focused, which is important to our employees and to me.

Advocate Health Advisors started in 2005, in large part because of the experience I had had with my mother. I mentioned the confusion we both faced when she turned sixty-five, around trying to navigate the healthcare system. After my friend helped get us squared away, I had to leave the country for a deployment. While I was away, someone from another insurance company met with my mom and enrolled her in a plan that was not suitable. When I returned and found out what had happened, I was deeply frustrated. The person who'd made the change to her policy was no longer with the company, which was unfortunate, because they had basically perpetrated a crime and gotten away with it. They sold her bad insurance.

Despite my aggravation with the situation, I also saw an opportunity. The baby boomer population is aging in staggering numbers and the community desperately needs guidance, just as my mother had. This is not pie-in-the-sky stuff. It's very real. It's very personal. These are real people facing real problems.

For example, one of our clients was ex-military and entitled to benefits through the US Department of Veterans Affairs (VA). It's no secret that the VA has challenges, but the doctor our client saw there told him he needed dialysis, which caused him a considerable amount of stress. He thought the end was near. Thankfully, he was on a Medicare Advantage Plan, which gave him access to an extended network of doctors to get a second opinion. He was told he did *not*, in fact, need dialysis, and the new doctor put him on a different treatment regimen that caused him to feel much better.

With a little bit of guidance and a few phone calls on our

client's behalf, we were able to sidestep the misery, cost, and stress associated with a long-term dialysis regimen. Instead, our client is healthier, wealthier, and happier. His healthcare options represented two sides of the same coin, and his story is exactly why we do what we do.

Advocate Health Advisors was launched with the intention of serving the greater good by fighting the battles that need to be fought—to do what needs to be done.

HOW TO WIN

Need to Know is a part of my mission to serve. I wrote it to give people the tools and information necessary to prepare for, fight, and win on the healthcare battlefield. What does "winning" look like for an aging population and those who care for them? Winning means living and dying on your own terms. It means leaving a legacy, not going into bankruptcy, and passing something on to your heirs if you choose to do so—even if that legacy is simply the example you set.

This book outlines the core information you need to know, in three parts. The first part defines the enemy. We'll look at the particulars of the industry, the nature of the known enemy, and then identify the surprise enemy. As Sun Tzu, a Chinese strategist, said, "Know your enemy and know yourself." The second part examines the three core tenets of arming yourself for the healthcare battle: nutrition, movement, and mindset. Part three focuses on the way forward. We'll talk about what's working and what's coming, and explore some of the exciting emerging technologies. Each chapter includes a few crucial "need to know" lessons, learned from my time in the military, that apply directly to the healthcare landscape.

A lack of knowledge and awareness leaves you vulnerable to attack from deadly diseases and chronic illnesses. The importance of educating oneself on the ins and outs of the healthcare system cannot be underestimated. The more you know, the better informed you are to make military-style decisions and be armed for battle. Education involves knowing what the landscape looks like and having awareness about what options and pitfalls are out there. Your knowledge and ability to navigate the terrain will have a direct impact on your happiness and overall well-being, and perhaps those of your loved ones as well.

Don't be caught off guard: mitigate the risk by being prepared. For example, UPS studied traffic patterns and accident incident reports to determine that there is a higher chance of getting into an accident when making a left-hand turn. As a result, they implemented a traffic control plan in which all UPS drivers primarily make right-hand turns.[12] This cuts down on the risk of accidents and

---

12   http://www.businessinsider.com/ups-efficiency-secret-our-trucks-never-turn-left-2011-3

keeps insurance premiums manageable. As an added bonus, it also saves millions of gallons of fuel each year and drastically reduces emissions.

By looking at the threat, UPS was able to mitigate the risk, and the same is possible when it comes to personal health. Make a plan with a multi-layered defense by knowing your own and your family's medical history. You have the power to decide how you will handle uncertainties down the road, and you can influence the outcome simply by being prepared.

Lives are won or lost based on the actions that you take now.

Navigating healthcare is hard. The battlefield is complicated, and the parameters are disjointed and constantly shifting. Nevertheless, we all have choices to make. When my mom was getting older, she wanted to continue living in her own home. I was in a tough spot because I wanted her to have the safety of a controlled environment where she would be well cared for around the clock. With some help, I was able to find home care that allowed my mom to live on her own terms. They weren't there 24/7, but they provided the level of care she needed in her own, comfortable environment. Ultimately, it came down to making the best decision that honored her wishes but also mitigated the risk of her getting hurt.

We're in this together, as a nation. It's a team sport, and we all have our roles. A winning team needs more than two players, the patient and the primary-care doctor. It needs an entire care team to go the distance and drive the ball down the field. Lives are saved when there is a strong, professional, interoperable team. That team involves all of the major players, not just the providers of care. It includes the individual, the provider, the health plan, the government, and the insurance agent. We all have a stake in the game. We are all *stakeholders*.

By acting together, we can extend quality of life, avoid misery, drive cost out of the equation, and improve overall peace of mind. The thoughts and decisions that you make today will have a direct impact on how you live and how you die. Don't leave your life to chance; get in the game.

Welcome to the team. Welcome to the fight.

PART I

THE
BATTLEFIELD

CHAPTER 1

WHAT IF I TOLD YOU THERE WAS A WAR?

NEED-TO-KNOW NUGGETS

- Healthcare is a battlefield.
- Your decisions matter.
- You have an obligation as a citizen, parent, or child.
- If you are stronger, the nation is stronger.

What if the United States was at war, and losing over 250,000 lives a year and spending trillions of dollars? The nation would be up in arms. Everyone would be concerned. The media would be working on overdrive. There would be demonstrations everywhere. Why do I ask? The sad truth is, that is exactly what is happening in the healthcare industry today. Each year, over 250,000 people die from medical errors. We are spending $3.3 trillion to pay for healthcare, one-third of which is wasted. The battle with healthcare far outweighs the casualties or costs of any other war this country has ever engaged in.[13]

Depending on which report you read, it is estimated that since 9/11, the combined cost of the wars in Iraq, Afghanistan, and other Global War on Terror operations has been $1.6 trillion.[14] The healthcare spending over the same time period is $25 trillion. We spend $3.3 trillion *every single year* on healthcare in the United States.[15] That's about seventeen times more per year on healthcare than on war in the last fifteen years. Furthermore, the number of amputees in Iraq and Afghanistan combined, over a ten-year period, equals approximately 1,645.[16] Yet, every year, there are 108,000[17] lower-extremities amputations in the US from type 2 diabetes alone, and 185,000[18] lower-extremities amputations total. The numbers are staggering.

Healthcare statistics of lives lost, expenses, and collective misery are exponentially worse than a war. We have a big problem on our hands, and it needs to be addressed

13   https://www.va.gov/opa/publications/factsheets/fs_americas_wars.pdf

14   https://fas.org/sgp/crs/natsec/RL33110.pdf

15   https://www.cms.gov/research-statistics-data-and-systems/statistics-trends-and-reports/
      nationalhealthexpenddata/nhe-fact-sheet.html

16   https://fas.org/sgp/crs/natsec/RS22452.pdf

17   https://www.cdc.gov/diabetes/pdfs/data/statistics/national-diabetes-statistics-report.pdf

18   https://www.amputee-coalition.org/limb-loss-resource-center/resources-filtered/
      resources-by-topic/limb-loss-statistics/limb-loss-statistics/#2

immediately. Every single citizen and their loved ones will eventually set foot on that healthcare battlefield. It's not a choice. You will be drafted. Most people already have been in one way or another, either by helping a sick relative or by dealing with the healthcare system directly.

MISSION ANALYSIS

When I was at Command and General Staff College, I learned about the Military Decision-Making Process (MDMP),[19] its history and evolution over time, and how to utilize it today. Militaries have studied this process since the times of ancient Greece to better understand why some leaders win and some lose. According to the manual, the MDMP is a single, established, and proven analytical process. The MDMP is an adaptation of the Army's analytical approach to problem solving. The MDMP is a tool that assists the commander and staff in developing estimates and a plan.

If two armies had the same training, the same soldiers, and the same equipment, the army that made the better decisions would win the battle. Better, faster decisions matter in war, and they matter in life. The best leaders are those who are able to make the best decisions and see them through.

A military mission is simply a problem that needs to be

---

19   http://www.au.af.mil/au/awc/awcgate/army/fm101-5_mdmp.pdf

solved. In solving that problem, the first step in the process is to receive or anticipate the receipt of a mission. The next part is to make sure you're aligned to higher headquarters, two echelons up. Think about connecting two dots. If you have two dots, you can place a third dot that is aligned with the other two. In the military, we call this being nested. It simply means we have unity of effort. The next step is to get into the details.

Mission analysis is when all of the information is evaluated. Historically, the enemy doctrine was to get behind our lines and cut off the flow of supplies, like bullets, water, and medicine. The enemy either wanted to punch a hole in the front lines or drop behind them. If we were trying to protect the area, we would look at all of the places they might enter. How many miles of road were there? Were there trains, fields, woods, or a place for airborne troops to land? All of the data related to the site and terrain were analyzed as part of the decision-making process.

Leaders who spend time on the front end of mission analysis perform more successfully than those who don't. They have a better handle on the various courses of action and all the variables, and an understanding of potential obstacles.

When I started to look at the healthcare industry, I tapped into my military background and used my mission-analysis training to examine the problems. I wanted to have a firm grasp on all the data and the landscape to more effectively identify the areas and people that needed the most help. Because of my military experience, I knew that getting the initial analysis correct would lead to a better solution.

Large industries have inefficiencies. They are almost inescapable, as anyone who has ever worked for a large corporation is probably aware, and on some level, they are to be expected. The healthcare industry's inefficiencies are of particular concern because of its sheer enormity as well as the threat it poses to national security due to the costs. So, let's do our own mission analysis of the healthcare industry.

THE LANDSCAPE OF THE INDUSTRY
THE PLAYERS

- 950,000 physicians (400,00 primary care and 450,000 specialists)[20]
- Approximately 5,600 hospitals[21]
- Over 4 million nurses[22]

---

20 https://www.kff.org/other/state-indicator/total-active-physicians/?currentTimeframe=0&sort
   Model=%7B%22colId%22:%22Location%22,%22sort%22:%22asc%22%7D

21 http://www.aha.org/research/rc/stat-studies/fast-facts.shtml

22 https://www.kff.org/other/state-indicator/total-registered-nurses/?currentTimeframe=0&sor
   tModel=%7B%22colId%22:%22Location%22,%22sort%22:%22asc%22%7D

- 327 million citizens[23]
- Approximately 4 million people turning 65 every year[24]
- 1.7 million life- and health-insurance agents[25]

USAGE

- $3.3 trillion spent annually
- 70 percent of healthcare costs are attributable to individual behaviors such as smoking, alcohol abuse, and obesity[26]
- 1 percent of the population accounted for 20.2 percent of total healthcare expenditures[27]
- 5 percent of patients are responsible for 50 percent of healthcare spending, with 25 percent of the costs occurring in the last year of life[28]

SOURCES OF WASTE—EXAMPLES[29]

- $210 billion in unnecessary services

---

23   https://www.census.gov/popclock/

24   https://money.usnews.com/money/blogs/on-retirement/2012/03/23/
     the-baby-boomer-number-game

25   https://adc.advisordatabases.com/Login.aspx

26   https://nahu.org/media/1147/healthcarecost-driverswhitepaper.pdf

27   https://meps.ahrq.gov/data_files/publications/st354/stat354.shtml

28   https://www.kff.org/medicare/issue-brief/medicare-spending-at-the-end-of-life/

29   Reprinted with permission from National Academy of Sciences, *Best Care at Lower Cost:
     The Path to Continuously Learning Health Care in America*, (2013), Courtesy of the National
     Academies Press, Washington, D.C.

- $190 billion in excessive administrative costs
- $130 billion in inefficiently delivered services
- $105 billion in overpriced services
- $75 billion in fraud
- $55 billion in missed prevention
- **Total: $765 billion**

Type 2 diabetes is largely preventable, and the consequences of the disease are every bit as severe and traumatic as those reaped on the battlefield. One of my managers in Puerto Rico told me that if there is such a thing as hell on earth, it is laser treatment for his diabetic retinopathy. He underwent the procedure while he was fully conscious. His eyes were open as wide as possible while the doctors worked on his retinal blood vessels to help his vision. He described the noise of the machines, the fear of the procedure while it was happening, and the overall misery of the entire experience. Hundreds of thousands of people endure these types of procedures due to diseases that are mostly preventable.

In addition to the misery and cost, there is another important category of waste in the healthcare system not listed earlier: wait time. For example, if a patient needs to see a specialist or make an appointment with a new primary care doctor, the timeline to get an appointment could be anywhere from three to six weeks.[30] Then, there is the wait time at the actual appointment. What's the longest amount of time you or a loved one has waited to get in to see the doctor for ten to fifteen minutes of his or her time?

If the patient needs to have tests or lab work done, even more time is added to the process. First, you have to make the appointment, then you actually have to go to the appointment, and then you have to schedule yet another appointment to get the results. The whole thing could take weeks. During the writing of this book, a friend of mine, Katie, was diagnosed with stage 3 melanoma. Eighteen months prior, she had had a spot removed that was confirmed to be melanoma. I am not sure what instructions were issued for follow-up, but eighteen months later there was a hugely swollen lymph node that ended up being stage 3 melanoma. Originally, the pathology lab had diagnosed melanoma, but they did not identify which type. When Katie arrived at the cancer center several weeks later, the oncologists could not choose a treatment plan without knowing exactly what type of melanoma it was. The cancer center was not able to conduct its own tests during the meeting to determine the specifics, and sent Katie home. Upon returning home, Katie called the lab to see if they had the details, but they were closed. So, she sat with life-threatening cancer in her body, wishing

---

30 https://www.merritthawkins.com/uploadedFiles/MerrittHawkins/Pdf/
    mha2017waittimesurveyPDF.pdf

it was gone, and anxiously waiting for a solution. She understood that the difference between stage 3 and stage 4 is the difference between life and death. Katie has three children, is a great mother with a loving husband, and leads a healthy lifestyle. She deserves better than this. We all do.

All of these inefficiencies don't factor the patient's time or energy into the equation. There is no accounting for how much worry and uncertainty goes into waiting for the results, or some answers, or a plan. The whole experience of waiting exacts a heavy toll on one's soul.

Personally, I have a very hard time with waste and inefficiency, which was one of the primary motivators for going into the healthcare industry. I think it goes back to when I was a child and my post-depression-era parents hated for me to waste food, or anything else. The lesson has stayed with me to this day. Some people like to clean and organize; I like to see efficiency. When I see people experience pain or misfortune unnecessarily, it makes me angry, especially if the issue is preventable or the person isn't aware of an easier or better way.

Everyone has their "thing," and ever since I was younger, mine has been efficiency. Sometimes, this drive can get in the way, but my intention is always to help and make things easier for people. For example, I was walking toward my car in Tampa one morning, and I saw a meter maid heading up the street. My car was not in danger of getting a ticket, but I could see several others up ahead with expired meters. I had a pocket full of change, so I started popping quarters and dimes into each slot. I do this kind of thing a lot, not because I'm looking for a Good Samaritan Award,[31] but because it saves people unnecessary headaches and it costs me very little. Unnecessary headaches drive me nuts. Some people make fun of me about it, but it's a primary driver behind what I do. I want to make things simpler, so people can live better lives.

THE NEED TO SIMPLIFY

The entire community of stakeholders needs to come together to promote prevention and avoid further misery. It's the only way to work efficiently. Currently, we are divided into distinct membership groups:

---

31 http://goodsamaritanawards.com/

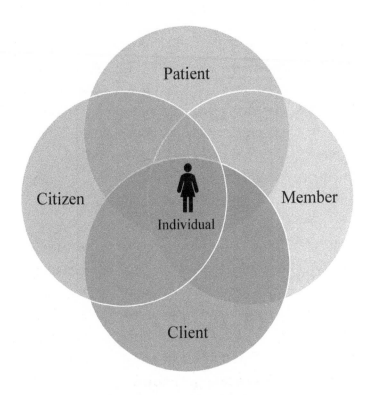

The four different groups each try to serve their own con-
stituents, but all of them are actually the same person: the
individual. The citizen the government is trying to protect
is also an insurance-company member, a doctor's patient,
and a health-insurance agent's client. Each group looks
at the same person from their own perspective, which is a
large part of the problem. The solution to the healthcare
battlefield lies in looking at everyone as a member of
one giant community of stakeholders. Everyone needs
to work together to be more proactive and less reactive.

The demographic facts could be viewed as a business

equation. Every year, five million people turn sixty-five and become eligible for Medicare. They live longer and get sicker all the time. The senior population consumes the largest amount of resources. There is a huge demand for a limited amount of supplies, and something's got to give. The problem needs to be addressed through a combination of enhanced preventative measures, increased efficiencies, and personal accountability.

In any other industry, the statistics would suffice to launch radical change. To drive cost out, first, we must understand the complexity of the problem. The numbers are scary and the people who are facing healthcare decisions are scared. People who are under stress tend to behave and make decisions differently than they would under normal circumstances. The information they receive from the doctors and insurance plans can be complicated. Simply knowing what needs to be done and when takes time and energy, and often people don't have the luxury of doing the necessary research to make an informed decision. Often, decisions need to be made quickly, and sometimes, it can be difficult to get a straight answer.

I recall being in the hospital with my mother once; the doctors requested that she get an MRI. I tried to find out the cost and no one could tell me. The cost depended on several variables that no one person had access to at the time: the insurance carrier's policy, the deductible, and the type of MRI ordered. It was a moment of extreme urgency and I was unable to get the answers I needed to make a decision. Under those circumstances, the tendency is to do nothing—or to do everything!

When people understand the complexity of the problem in advance, it is easier to demystify it. Through demystification, it becomes possible to arm yourself for battle through research and education, which then lead to more proactive and empowered decision making. When you can navigate the system to best meet your own needs or the needs of your loved ones, you are less likely to be processed through the system like a piece of meat.

The only way to drive cost out of the equation is through improved efficiencies and prevention. The necessary efficiencies will come when people are no longer viewed as clients, patients, citizens, or plan members, but as individuals. The government, the doctors, the health plans, and the agents are there to help and serve a community of individuals.

A CALL TO ARMS

There is a strong sense of urgency surrounding the healthcare battlefield. When you face your own mortality, as we all will do, priorities tend to shift into order, which impacts the way you live now. To survive as long as possible on your own terms, you need to become an active participant in your own care and make better choices about your health. You must understand the battlefield to make the right choices: pick the right doctor, navigate the system, and know your metrics.

Everyone, the world over, has a unique and personal story about someone who got sick, someone who is currently struggling, or someone in their own house who is on the battlefield fighting every day. No matter where I go, people have health or sickness stories. I often hear, "My father has type 2 diabetes. He doesn't take care of himself the way I wish he would. It's becoming unmanageable." Many people feel alone or isolated by their own health problems or those of others, but the truth is that everyone is dealing with health problems on some level. Baby boomers are aging all over the world; they're living longer than ever and they're living with more disease.[32]

Death and loss are very hard, but they can be less so if we are prepared. Both the person who is dying and the people around them will have a calmer and more peaceful experience of death when they are ready for it.

THE ADVANTAGES OF PREPARATION

I had a training experience in the army that modeled

---

32 https://www.census.gov/prod/2014pubs/p25-1140.pdf

how people should prepare for the healthcare battle at home. The army discovered decades ago that soldiers fight the way they are trained. When I was getting ready to go over to Bosnia, we had to plan and prepare for how to handle land mines, which were scattered randomly and abundantly throughout the country.

We learned everything there is to know about land mines before we left the US. We learned to probe for land mines, watched videos to see what happens when they detonate, learned how they are made, and met with and talked to people who had been dismembered as a result of them. Ultimately, before stepping foot in Bosnia, we had a profound understanding of what we were up against as well as the consequences that land mines are capable of creating.

The reality of land mines was drilled into us on every level imaginable. We trained in different environments and under multiple scenarios. To this day, I have a heightened sense of awareness when I stand on the side of a road because of how efficiently I was trained for Bosnia. This awareness continued during my career, all the way through my last tour in Afghanistan with what we now call improvised explosive devices (IED). My behavior was forever modified as a result.

If we apply the same level of focused training and learning to the healthcare system, we will all be significantly better prepared to go to war. The life-and-death consequences are the same, even though no one wants to talk about them. Most organizations shy away from the unpleasantness of death, despite the fact that it is inevitable. Politicians and corporations want to sugarcoat the truth, but they are fighting a losing battle. Communication is key to a winning battle plan.

Even the healthcare industry tiptoes around the truth. We use nice terms like "preventive services." No one is saying, "You know what? Getting your colon checked sounds a lot worse than it is. But if you don't do it, even though you are supposed to, you could end up living with a bag or dying from colon cancer." Our society simply does not work that way, but it should.

If we open the lines of communication and help our citizens and patients be proactive about their healthcare, we can save ourselves untold amounts of misery and money. Outcomes will be different when people hear a clearer message.

The communication norms of our culture, particularly in corporate America, favor nicety over reality. People speak to each other one level kindlier than they really are at their core. For example, if someone does an average job, they are praised and told, "Great job, Mike!" Very rarely is someone told their performance is average or below expectation, unless it was terrible.

In the military, on the other hand, clear and candid communication is embraced, appreciated, and expected. There is a high standard for success which is not always achieved through niceties. The consequences of miscommunication could easily be a matter of life and death. There is no time to mince words in a confusing or dire circumstance. The healthcare industry could benefit by adapting a new cultural norm and embracing clarity and candor in all matters. The truth can be hard to dish out, and even harder to handle, but it is an absolute necessity when facing the casualties of war.

CHAPTER 2

CASUALTIES OF WAR

Diseases attack you just like a terrorist or mugger attacks you. The difference is that many diseases are predictable, and a lot is known about them. To avoid being a casualty of this war, you need to use that knowledge and take the situation seriously, as if you're entering combat.

TAKE IT SERIOUSLY AND BE PREPARED

If you went to war, and you were stepping onto the battlefield, you'd be prepared—because if you were not prepared, your odds of surviving would plummet.

We probably all learned about the concept of "fight or flight," which was originally described by Walter Bradford Cannon in the early 1900s.[33] Later, the Special Operations Command and the FBI conducted a very interesting study. What they found is that in certain circumstances, such as when someone is put in a stressful situation, the body initiates the "fight or flight" mechanism. You may freeze up for a few seconds, as if you're coming under attack. But they also found that training and preparation make a difference. If you're properly trained and prepared, you can instinctively spring into action. In other words, when the environment causes you to be overwhelmed, most people become temporarily gridlocked and paralyzed. But those who have had training about what to do spring into action faster.

I have a friend, Cullen, who's a retired police officer. He used to run the police firing range at Charlotte-Mecklenburg after his time on the SWAT team. Part of his job during training was to put the maximum amount of stress on officers during training, to prepare them for the most stressful situations they might face in the field. He knows his stuff, down to the exact heart rate he needs

---

33 Walter Bradford Cannon, *Bodily Changes in Pain, Hunger, Fear, and Rage* (New York: Appleton-Century-Crofts, 1929).

to get them to in order to ensure maximum stress. In other words, he put them into "fight or flight" mode and would watch as a different part of their brain took over the decision-making process.

During the training, while police were shooting, moving from target to target amid smoke and strobe lights, Cullen would be yelling at them. "Reload! Reload!" he would yell and watch as they took whatever he handed them—TV remote control, shotgun shell—and tried to jam it into their gun where the magazine was supposed to go. On one occasion, he gave them a candy bar and watched as they loaded it into the gun, tried to fire, then pulled the candy bar out and reloaded it, trying to make it work a second time.

Similarly, people today feel overwhelmed by their health problems and by the system. Fight or flight kicks in, and they don't fight. They don't feel empowered because they don't understand their own health, and they don't understand the system. The tendency—the "flight response"—is to just hope things will get better. My favorite quote from former Army Chief of Staff Gordon R. Sullivan's book might be the title itself: *Hope Is Not a Method*. Being passive and unengaged in the process won't help you.

When people feel overwhelmed, they often feel disempowered. They become passive rather than active. For example, when seniors go into the doctor's office, they often don't ask the most important questions because they're overwhelmed and intimidated. They're hoping the system will take care of them. Not realizing the power they have, they turn to what's called *bargaining behavior*. They think if they're submissive and don't cause any problems, maybe they'll get a better prognosis.

Many people, especially seniors, also tend to simply trust whatever the doctor says. Because of this, they just listen. I'm a big fan of doctors. I've got friends who are doctors, and I respect them greatly. However, that doesn't mean we can't question them. But we don't. We just trust them because they're doctors. We deify them. They have certainly earned the respect we tend to give them, but that doesn't mean they're godlike.

Instead, people should feel empowered when talking with their primary-care physician. Patients should feel comfortable and prepared for that conversation and have a checklist of things they're documenting so they can work with their doctor and render a better prognosis. Individuals should understand the power they do have, and the right they have to exercise it. We need to realize that we are on the same team as the doctor, fighting the same battle. Being active in your care and knowing what you need to be prepared with helps avoid the unnecessary suffering of feeling powerless.

I understand the stress and worry that comes from a health concern, and what it takes to overcome it. After my biological mother died of pancreatic cancer, I knew I should get a sonogram of my pancreas as part of my annual checkup. Now, I'm a fairly successful person—and I know the risks, fear, and sacrifice it takes to succeed. I've been in combat. I've seen a lot and done a lot, and even I went into that sonogram with anxiety. I didn't want to know. I didn't even want to be there. But I did it. And afterward, when the doctors told me everything was fine, I felt the relief that comes with hearing that kind of news. I had a weight lifted off my shoulders, because now I knew for certain the state of my health—at least at that moment in time.

People do irrational things under stress—even if we're not talking about combat, where bullets are flying or you're kicking in a door without knowing who's behind it. Stress is stress. In your own world, a healthcare crisis is probably the biggest—and most stressful—event that's going to happen to you in any particular year. Becoming engaged in your own healthcare and preparing for situations is what will help you to avoid being overwhelmed by the system. When you can avoid being overwhelmed, you can avoid unnecessary stress. And when you can avoid unnecessary stress, you can take the necessary action.

To take necessary action, first we need to be prepared.

LIFE EXPECTANCY AND CAUSES OF DEATH

Looking at causes of death is a good start to being prepared. Today, the life expectancy in the US is approximately seventy-nine years. If you turn sixty-five today, you can expect about fourteen more years.[34] But that's just an average. There's a lot of geographic disparity. For people in certain counties in the southeastern US, average life expectancy is sixty-seven years old.[35] And in certain counties in California and Colorado, which have the highest life expectancy in the country, it's eighty-seven—a disparity of twenty years! As we'll see, the choices you make in your lifestyle are profound. They can guard against the enemy or welcome it in. What's out to get you? Heart disease is out to get you. Cancer is out to get you. And it doesn't stop there.

Many of the leading causes of death are preventable.[36] Yes, you should know your family history and where you're more vulnerable, but it's not just your genetics. Genetics load the gun, but your environment pulls the trigger. Why do some people live to be sixty-seven and others eighty-seven? Sure, some of that difference is genetic, but we wouldn't have that geographic disparity if the environment

34 https://www.census.gov/prod/2014pubs/p25-1140.pdf

35 Rob Stein, "Life Expectancy Can Vary By 20 Years Depending On Where You Live," National Public Radio, May 8, 2017, https://www.npr.org/sections/health-shots/2017/05/08/527103885/life-expectancy-can-vary-by-20-years-depending-on-where-you-live

36 https://www.cdc.gov/mmwr/pdf/wk/mm6317.pdf

didn't play a role. And there are a lot of environmental factors. It's where you live—or lived. Your lifestyle choices: What you eat. How (and how much) you move your body. Your mindset. There are a lot of things you can control, and the first step to controlling them is to educate yourself.

Here are the leading causes of death in the United States of America for the years 1900[37] and 2015,[38] according to the Centers for Disease Control and Prevention (CDC):

LEADING CAUSES OF DEATH IN THE UNITED STATES OF AMERICA

Ranking	Causes of Death (1900)	Deaths	Causes of Death (2015)	Deaths
1	Pneumonia (All Forms) and Influenza	40,362	Heart Disease	633,842
2	Tuberculosis (All Forms)	38,820	Cancer	595,930
3	Diarrhea, Enteritis, and Ulceration of the	28,491	Respiratory Diseases	155,041
4	Diseases of the Heart	27,427	Accidents	146,571
5	Intracranial Lesions of Vascular Origin	21,353	Strokes	140,323
6	Nephritis (All Forms)	17,699	Alzheimer's	110,561
7	All Accidents	14,429	Diabetes	79,535
8	Cancer and Other Malignant Tumors	12,769	Influenza and Pneumonia	57,062
9	Senility	10,015	Nephritis, Nephrotic Syndrome, and Nephro	49,959
10	Diphtheria	8,056	Suicide	44,193

It is interesting how, over time, the causes of death have changed. Say what you will about the pharmaceutical companies, but they made a big difference. When was the last time you met someone who had polio or tuberculosis? How many people have you met who are in an iron lung? What will the causes of death over the next hundred years look like? In the future, I think we will view aging as a disease and list it as a cause of death. We label these

---

37   1900–1945 Tables Ranked in National Office of Vital Statistics, December 1947.

38   https://www.cdc.gov/nchs/fastats/leading-causes-of-death.htm

causes of death, but the truth is the cause goes deeper than the disease. Underlying many of these are the true causes, such as smoking and obesity.

Slips and falls, type 2 diabetes, and many other things are largely preventable. If you talk to a medical doctor or a coroner, or if you know somebody who works in a morgue, here's what they'll tell you: it might have been a heart attack or stroke that finally killed somebody, but that's not what really brought them to their end. My friend Matt works in an emergency room and tells me the people he sees are not typically the same people you see working out at the YMCA.

What's not shown in the top ten, but should be, is that medical errors are the number *three* cause of death. According to Johns Hopkins Medicine, medical errors account for more than 250,000 deaths in the US each year.[39] That's almost *10 percent of all deaths in the US*. Imagine if the military had a fratricide (death by friendly fire) rate of 10 percent. Would anyone stand for that? No way. If ten out of one hundred lodgers walked into a hotel to find someone in their own bed, would that hotel stay open? Not a chance.

Keep in mind that these errors aren't all as obvious as it might seem. It's not usually a case of the doctor cutting

---

39   https://hub.jhu.edu/2016/05/03/medical-errors-third-leading-cause-of-death/

the wrong thing. It's the system. It's fragmented care; it's doctors and other professionals missing things that could have been caught; it's someone's mom who didn't get some preventative checks when she should have, which could have saved her life. If you don't know what questions to ask, and what errors to make sure are avoided, you're at risk.

If we are going to count medical errors, it is only fair to consider another factor that doesn't show up in official statistics: what's known as *non-compliant behavior*. That's when the fault lies more with the patient—when patients don't do what their doctor told them to do, or don't take care of themselves in the first place. We're already battling diseases and the entire healthcare system. We shouldn't be battling ourselves as well.

ASSESSING AND MITIGATING RISK AND VULNERABILITY

There are two concepts related to mitigating your risk that I learned through the military. The first one is the *risk assessment*,[40] which is routinely done in the military as part of the planning process. When assessing risk, you start by looking at possible *consequences* and sorting them into three categories: low, mid, and high. The high end means the consequences could be catastrophic. Someone could die. If you're going to the range to shoot weapons, for example, someone *could* die.

40 https://www.rand.org/content/dam/rand/pubs/tools/TL100/TL129/RAND_TL129.pdf

Next, you look at the *probability* of a consequence happening. Is it low, medium, or high? In the same instance of a range operation, there's a low probability someone would die—but if that did happen, it would be catastrophic. Putting the consequences and probability together gives you a *risk level*. Assessing your risk is important because you are identifying possible problems and then taking steps to avoid them. For example, if you decide shooting at night is too dangerous, you may reduce the risk by shooting during the daytime.

The idea behind modifying the solution is to mitigate the risk. Note that you don't start out with risk mitigation. You start out by saying, "What's the problem?" and then work toward answering, "What's the solution?" Only after you define the solution do you consider how to mitigate the risk inherent in the solution. By contrast, sometimes government entities make rules to protect citizens by looking at risk mitigation first. If you do that, you could accidentally rule out some of the best solutions.

It's a well-intended effort, but it means the whole system will have to work around those rules, which may have been formulated before considering the best solution to the problem. In healthcare, that's problematic. We have to think about how to best care for the patient within the context of solving a problem and then worry about privacy or liability issues. Do you want your doctor to not perform a procedure based on liability versus what is in your best interest? Do you want your specialist to make a decision without a key piece of information because your privacy was protected?

The second concept I'm borrowing from the military is called a *vulnerability assessment*, in which you look at what's the most likely thing that is going to happen if you're vulnerable. If you're defending a base, for example, the first thing you might do is ask, "How would I attack this if I were attacking it?" In other words, you think about the situation from the opposite point of view. If I attack this particular way, what's the most likely thing that's going to happen? When you think about ways to defend something, your defense should be in layers. Think about your body. You don't just have one single defense against things like disease and injury—your body has multiple layers of defenses. In healthcare, we also want to ask, "What's likely to happen?"

Let's take an example. What's something that happens often that's avoidable? Consider people slipping and falling. People slip and fall every day, and a lot of really bad things happen as a result. Mobility and positive mindset often go down the tubes. You can argue that slips and falls are largely preventable.

I watch how people walk, seeing how steady they are (or

aren't). It's amazing how far a little physical therapy could go toward preventing slips and falls. Somebody who is not walking steadily and confidently might just need some physical therapy. They could do some fairly easy strength conditioning and balance work to help them walk better. This is low-hanging fruit, something that everybody sees but nobody does anything about. It's obvious. It's not complicated. It's not expensive. And it's a problem that's here, right now.

Each person should conduct their own vulnerability assessment and come up with their own battle plan. Each person should formulate and take their own defensive measures, based on their own vulnerability assessment. Where are your weak points? Is it your diet? Mobility? Are there steps you should take to combat your genetics? Whatever it is, it's necessary to think about how you might be attacked and create a defensive plan.

DISEASE AS THE ENEMY

In a vulnerability assessment, you want to protect something. Before someone robs a bank, they case the joint. Terrorists conduct surveillance, usually driving by and taking pictures. There's a process they go through to do the bad things they want to do: they look for weaknesses. So do diseases. Our job is to make sure they don't find any weaknesses.

One thing we can do is watch out for metrics we know are indicators that something is going to happen. If you're in a tower protecting a base and you see the same car come up three times in a month and take photographs, that's probably an indicator that something's happening. Indicators are clues, and you want to be aware of those clues. With your body, these clues can be found in metrics. You need to know what those metrics are because you want to know when things are going in the wrong direction. Just like that terrorist sitting shotgun taking pictures, it's a sign something bad will happen if you don't take action.

Think of diseases as terrorists and villains. Cancer is out there, driving by, taking pictures, looking for a chink in your armor so it can get you. Adopt the mindset that diseases are nefarious characters, plotting and calculating to rob you of your life, your energy, your vitality, your motivation, your joy—all of it. That's what's at risk, and that's what you need to defend. Diseases have a plan, and they're out to get you.

You need a plan too.

USING HEALTH TO COMBAT SICKNESS

The FBI has caught countless homegrown plots in the planning stages. Similarly, with cancer, scientists are finding that there are clues within your body regarding the predisposition or formation of cancer long before it happens. The most obvious clue is for colon cancer. Doctors can conduct a colonoscopy and see by the shape and the size of a polyp if it is eventually going to turn into cancer. If it is, they remove it. Research now suggests that 50 percent of colorectal cancers in the United States each year are preventable through diet, weight, and physical activity.[41] That's not too high a price to pay for the potential consequences. The same principle goes for screenings for breast cancer and multiple other diseases. The enemy acts over time. This means that, like the FBI does with terrorists, you can often catch these things in the planning stages and prevent them. And if they still make it through your defenses, you're better prepared to manage and eventually stop them.

FINDING YOUR COURSE OF ACTION

Remember, once you complete the mission analysis, you come up with a few different courses of action to accomplish that mission. The commander will then pick one, and that becomes the *operation order* that is executed. The people who are more successful on their missions are those who frontload the mission analysis. That's why I spent so much time on it in Chapter 1. For the individual, your own mission analysis includes facts about your

---

41   http://www.aicr.org/press/press-releases/2016/6_Steps_to_Prevent_Half_of_US_Colorectal_
Cancer_Cases.html

lifestyle, environment, family history, and genome. All that helps form the foundation of your own wellness plan.

So, first, know your enemy. You've got to know what's lurking out there: the known causes of death and their underpinnings, and obvious remedies like quitting smoking and reducing obesity. Know the risks of medical errors and engaging in noncompliant behaviors. Educate yourself on how the industry works (reading this book is a great start on that). Next, know yourself. Know your family history and how you're doing in the areas that can have an impact for diet, exercise, and the care model you're involved in. Those are all the raw ingredients and the basic tenets that you need to put together as you create your own plan.

CULTIVATING A SENSE OF URGENCY

You don't want to be a casualty of this war. As established in the Introduction and Chapter 1, the healthcare battlefield involves life-and-death consequences of such a magnitude that they dwarf recent American military conflicts. We're talking about World War II-level casualty rates, and then some.

We certainly wouldn't accept such errors in any other industry. We would never accept that level of inefficiency. The airline industry would end if it had as many accidents as the healthcare industry. Note that the airline industry is a self-reporting industry. I was flying recently, and the tower made a mistake. One of the alerts went off. Our plane was on a collision course with another plane. What happened? The warning systems worked, the pilots communicated, and the threat was averted. There's a form they fill out for the FAA in an incident like that.[42] It's commonplace in that industry to report every mishap of any sort. That's why the safety record in aviation is so good. They all work together and share information—lives are at stake, and so it is considered urgent that they do so. Why not in healthcare?

Unlike in the aviation industry, many medical errors are never reported. There are all sorts of liability issues in the healthcare industry, along with controversy about whether medical liability should be loosened or tightened up. But the fundamental problem is that many problems in healthcare are hidden and you don't hear about them. If we're not seeing ourselves as we are, it's going to be hard to make us better.

Another reason for a sense of urgency is that these diseases unfairly attack certain segments of our population more than others. If you look at any of the leading health indicators from the Department of Health and Human

---

42 https://asrs.arc.nasa.gov/overview/summary.html

Services' Healthy People 2020[43] or 2030[44] initiatives, you can see how the most vulnerable people are impacted by diseases the hardest. Lower-income people are being hardest hit, and they are the ones who need the most help.

Smoking is a simple example. The lower your education level and the lower your income level, the higher your probability of smoking.[45] You see this time and time again in place after place. Again, the people being victimized are the least able to care for themselves—they need somebody to help them. That's one reason I wrote this book.

I would put some of the older population in this category too. The elderly are the largest group of consumers of healthcare services. A small percentage of them are consuming the most services and yet, at the same time, are the least able to help themselves. The sad fact is that the lower your income and education, the worse your health and healthcare outcomes tend to be.[46] The natural evolution of the body is to die, and as it heads into those final days, you become weaker and more vulnerable. In the old days, you probably lived on a farm, got sick, and died. It was a

43 https://www.healthypeople.gov/

44 https://www.healthypeople.gov/2020/About-Healthy-People/
    Development-Healthy-People-2030

45 https://www.kff.org/disparities-policy/issue-brief/
    beyond-health-care-the-role-of-social-determinants-in-promoting-health-and-health-equity/

46 https://www.kff.org/disparities-policy/issue-brief/
    beyond-health-care-the-role-of-social-determinants-in-promoting-health-and-health-equity/

fairly quick process. It happened over a few weeks. Not so today, when the end of life gets drawn out and ends up costing a fortune, when, ironically, the person may have wanted to die in peace at home in their own bed. That's what most people really want, to die in peace at home versus the discomfort of multiple visits to the emergency room and thousands of dollars in medical bills.

My own sense of urgency comes from the fact that a whole segment of the population is at greater risk for life-and-death consequences, yet they're the ones least equipped to protect themselves. I want to help them. I feel an obligation to protect these people because they're not able to. In military terms, it's as if they're about to go into harm's way and they're ill-prepared for it. If they have a family member or a friend like you or me, we can help them. Remember the simple example of you or somebody you know who may be walking unsteadily. You can do something as simple as search the internet for exercises to do to make the muscles stronger. I once had to go through strenuous rehab for my back and shoulder pain. I now realize that if I'd done many of those rehab exercises in advance, I probably could have avoided the therapy and rehab altogether. I could have done a fraction of it on the front end and maybe never had the back pain or the shoulder injury to begin with. But back then, I didn't do what I should have been doing because I didn't know. I wasn't prepared for battle, and I paid the price—perhaps a small price compared to others, but a good lesson all the same.

Don't make the same kind of mistake. Now is your chance to get ahead of things. Assess your risk and vulnerability, formulate a plan to mitigate those things, get informed, determine your course of action, and use wellness to fight the enemy. You don't have to be a casualty of this war.

Speaking of the enemy, there's actually more than one, as you'll see in the next chapter.

CHAPTER 3

ANOTHER ENEMY: THE HEALTHCARE SYSTEM

NEED-TO-KNOW NUGGETS

- The system has not fully evolved to meet the changing needs of the population.
- The healthcare industry does not behave like any other industry.
- Military lessons learned can be applied to our current healthcare system.

As you read in Chapter 2, the obvious enemy is disease. This chapter is about a hidden enemy: the healthcare system itself. It's a complicated landscape. Battling and preventing diseases is bad enough, but unfortunately, the system that's supposed to help you actually works *against* you, and at a time when you're at your weakest. It's a system that can cure or kill you.

Chapter 1 mentioned the waste in the system, along with the fact that hundreds of people die every day unnecessarily. We shouldn't blame doctors, nurses, or the technology. I'm talking about something bigger than they are: the entire system itself. For example, consider the Veterans Health Administration (the VHA), which is one of the three components of the US Department of Veterans Affairs (the VA).

As reported by CNN, Thomas Breen was a seventy-one-year-old Navy veteran so proud of his service that, when he saw blood in his urine, he refused to go anywhere but the VHA for his treatment.[47] His son pleaded with him to get treatment sooner from a doctor elsewhere, but Breen trusted the system, as every American should be able to do. After an initial visit to the emergency room, in which his condition was called "urgent," Breen went home to await a follow-up appointment with a specialist. Some time went by, and he went back, trying to get in to see a doctor, but was told to be patient and was sent back home.

Seven months later, the VHA finally called to set up that "urgent" appointment, but it was too late. Breen had died of bladder cancer while waiting for the treatment he deserved.

---

47   http://www.cnn.com/2014/04/23/health/veterans-dying-health-care-delays/

He wasn't alone. The inspector general at the time said that about 1,700 veterans were "at risk of being forgotten or lost."[48] It was reported that the VHA was more than 45,000[49] clinical vacancies short, forcing them to send patients outside the VA system and costing taxpayers almost $8 billion.[50]

Veterans have earned their benefits, and there's a system in place to provide those benefits, but it's not getting the job done. It's a study in miniature of how the healthcare system fails us.

OPERATION EAGLE CLAW

In the last days of the Carter administration, just before Reagan came in, there were fifty-two American hostages being held in Iran. Operation Eagle Claw, a mission in which the Army, Marines, and the Air Force all worked together, was designed to free those hostages. Without going into a lot of detail, there was a sandstorm that led to a crash involving a plane and a helicopter. Eight servicemen died, and there was no hostage rescue. An investigation

---

detailed in the Holloway Report[51] later revealed that the systems the different military units used in the operation didn't talk to each other. The services didn't train together. There were command and control problems: there was no identifiable command post on scene, teams didn't know each other, and instructions had to be questioned until proper authority could be established.

The military groups involved were world-class. There was nobody better in the world at doing what they did, yet they still suffered that crash and those deaths, and they never accomplished their mission of freeing the hostages. But there is a silver lining. Out of the ashes and that loss of life, the multiservice organization United States Special Operations Command was created. The military learned a hard lesson about interoperability and took action. Under the US Special Operations Command, the special operators now work in a unified way. Teams of multiple services—Army, Navy, Air Force, Marines, and Coast Guard—work seamlessly together as one community.

This is a great analogy for what our healthcare system needs to do. We have the best doctors and health professionals in the world. Surgeons and advanced specialists are the healthcare equivalent of Delta Force. Nurses and other caregivers are like the co-pilots and the air crew that make things happen. But they're part of a system that

---

51 https://nsarchive2.gwu.edu/NSAEBB/NSAEBB63/doc8.pdf

doesn't allow them to work together the way they need to. Unlike the way the military learned from and adapted from Operation Eagle Claw, the American healthcare system has yet to do the same. That lack of transformation has tremendous consequences.

THE HEALTHCARE INDUSTRY DOESN'T BEHAVE LIKE ANY OTHER INDUSTRY

The healthcare system simply hasn't evolved in terms of the ability to shop for and buy services based on value, efficiency, and customer service.

We don't get to be good shoppers in our healthcare system. And what's more, we may not even realize we should be shopping for our own healthcare. Usually when we make an important purchase, we shop. If I need a new roof, I'll get a couple of estimates. If I want a new car, I may go to more than one dealership. American healthcare doesn't come with price tags, let alone allow you to comparison shop. And that doesn't even consider whose money you are spending.

Today, in our third-party payer system, someone else pays your healthcare bill. You might pay a premium or a co-pay but, generally speaking, someone else, like an insurance company or the government, pays the remainder of the bill. As you might guess, some individuals tend to spend another person's money differently than their own. Imagine your teenager needs a car. Would you say, "Hey, go buy a car and send me the bill" or would you say, "Here's $12,000. Let's shop together to find the best car for you that we can"? You would probably end up with two very different vehicles. Unfortunately, that's how our healthcare system largely works today. You go to the doctor and someone else gets the bill.

And how did you pick that doctor anyhow? How do you know how good your doctor is? Based on their experience? Their stellar track record of outcomes? The fact is that people pick the doctor down the street. There's no Consumer Reports or Trip Advisor-like app commonly used to pick a physician.

The inability to shop for and buy services based on value is a fundamental problem. As we solve that problem, other things will take care of themselves.

Now consider efficiency. If the doctor writes me a prescription and I have to go drop it off at the pharmacy, and the pharmacy can't fill it right then, I have to leave the pharmacy and go do something else. Now I'm on their time, not mine. Since I'm waiting, I try to go about my life and get distracted by all the things I need to do, and I don't have the chance to get back until it's too late and they're closed. Now I'm not taking the medicine I need because I'm busy working and living my life, and I still have to go all the way back there once again to wait in line to buy it. It's ridiculous.

What frustrates me even more is when I go to the walk-in clinic, for the seventh time, and they ask me if I have been here before. When I say "yes," they look in the system, tell me it's been over a month, and that I will need to fill out some forms. So, I get a clipboard with several pieces of paper to fill out, of which half are related to liability and privacy, and the other half force me to recite not only my own entire medical history, but that of my parents. Yet again! If my life relies on my memory or how well I fill out those forms, I am in real trouble.

Customer service and satisfaction are not exactly at the forefront either. If you've ever been admitted to a hospital, you know that a hospital may be good at keeping you alive, but it's not very good at making you comfortable. They're on their schedule. Again, let me add here how great these individual people are. They're nice, proficient, and caring, but *you* are definitely fitting into *their* world. The good news, however, is that if you go into the hospital (setting aside medical errors and other circumstances), you'll probably live even if you are not comfortable. Still, it's not like going to a hotel. In some places, that's changing, and the model is evolving, but overall, it's just not there yet.

If you haven't already, you really need to see the 1951 movie *People Will Talk*, with Cary Grant as Dr. Praetorius. The character wonders whether the practice of medicine will "become more and more intimately involved with the human beings it treats or whether it is to go on in its present way of becoming more and more a thing of pills, serums and knives until eventually there is an undoubtedly evolved electronic doctor."

Let's consider two other examples. Nowadays, you go around the world and put your ATM card in a machine, get your balance, and withdraw your money in the local currency. The ATM I use not only remembers me, it knows what denominations I prefer. Yet getting my consolidated medical record to anyone remains a major undertaking.

Heck, look at pizza. I called to order a pizza the other day, and they said, "Oh, Mr. Hale. Is it soccer day again? Are you going to get eighteen pepperoni pizzas?" I said, "No, the soccer team isn't here. I just want mine." They say, "Oh, okay." They know what I've ordered before. They know my history. It's personal. They also ask questions and anticipate things and get me that pizza in a half hour or so.

The healthcare system simply must evolve to improve the ability to shop, to become more efficient, and to elevate the overall customer experience. And it *is* transforming, but it's transforming very slowly—in my view, mostly due to the consumer's inability to shop for value.

FROM EPISODIC CARE TO CHRONIC CARE

The United States began as an agrarian society. In the early to late 1700s, 90 percent of the population were farmers.[52] And, as farmers, we worked outside all day and of course grew our own food. People basically lived and died on the farm, and when they died, it was a fairly quick onset and often didn't take too long. When it was their time, it was their time.

That model persisted for a long time. Even during the Industrial Revolution of the 1800s, as people moved off the farm, more than 90 percent of the steel used in the United States still went to farm-related products and equipment, but other things were changing.[53] We discovered how to improve the appearance and shelf life of many foods with manmade chemicals. We began to process food and learned to trick our taste buds by manipulating the fat, salt, and sugar content—it was worse for us, but tasted good, lasted longer, cost less, and we ate more and more of it. That trend continued throughout the twentieth century until it reached the very advanced level we see today. The food supply has changed.

---

52   https://www.agclassroom.org/gan/timeline/farmers_land.htm

53   http://www.nber.org/chapters/c1567.pdf

Now, we have the digital revolution, and, on top of consuming all these processed foods, we're sitting in front of screens for long periods of time. We're not working our bodies and moving them as they were made to move. The result of all this is that the health of the population has been transformed. We've seen a lot of chronic diseases emerge. People are living longer thanks to science and technology, but they are also getting more illnesses that must be treated with even *more* science and technology.

We've gone from the need for episodic care to the need for chronic care. If you got hurt on the farm—say a horse kicked you or you cut yourself on the plow—the doctor would come out to the farm and patch you up. That was episodic care, responding to an episodic event at a specific moment in time. Most diseases were incurable, and if they led to death, it didn't take too long.

Now, we have a population where, according to the National Council on Aging, 80 percent of the people over age sixty-five have a chronic condition, and 68 percent of the population have two or more of these chronic conditions.[54] These include high blood pressure (58 percent of the sixty-five-plus population), high cholesterol (47 percent), coronary heart disease (29 percent), diabetes (27 percent), and several others.[55] The model of care needed

---

54 https://www.ncoa.org/healthy-aging/chronic-disease/

55 https://www.ncoa.org/blog/10-common-chronic-diseases-prevention-tips/

to treat these chronic conditions is known as chronic care. Chronic problems require chronic care, and chronic care requires the coordination of caregivers and involves anticipating and predicting what's likely to happen. Multiple doctor visits per year are necessary. Patients need preventative checks, management programs, and pharmaceutical drugs. The medical needs of the population are different for chronic than for episodic care, and we've only just begun this transition to that new model.

THE FLEXNER REPORT

In the early 1990s, medical professionals recognized there were problems in healthcare delivery and in the teaching in medical schools. The quality of healthcare varied too much throughout the country. In 1910, Abraham Flexner published a book-length study of the healthcare system, in association with the Carnegie Foundation. The Flexner Report called for higher admissions and graduation standards in medical schools. It recommended protocols to ensure that medical schools were teaching a consistent curriculum and concluded that there were too many medical schools. For example, it said that Chicago's fourteen medical schools were "a disgrace to the state whose laws permit its existence."[56] It went on to describe conditions

---

56 Abraham Flexner, *Medical Education in the United Stated and Canada* (Princeton, NJ: Carnegie Foundation for the Advancement of Teaching, 1910).

as "the plague spot of the country."[57] In another example, the author was observing exams and asked the professor why he was giving oral exams. The professor replied that it was because many of his students "could barely read and write."[58]

The report had a major impact in the medical field, revealing it to be in disarray. In the report's wake, a number of new standards were put in place, and the number of medical schools and medical school graduates were cut by roughly half.[59] The prerequisites for medical school were increased. Physicians were trained in the scientific method. State regulation of medical licenses was strengthened. Medical schools gained control over many hospitals, so there was good clinical instruction in hospitals.

While the Flexner Report also created some controversy—many doctors who were taken out of the system were African American, women were still not allowed to practice, and there were fewer doctors—these reforms set the foundations for the system we have today. The medical schools that met Flexner's standards became the origins of our current system. In fact, today's medical schools

---

57 Abraham Flexner, *Medical Education in the United Stated and Canada* (Princeton, NJ: Carnegie Foundation for the Advancement of Teaching, 1910).

58 Abraham Flexner, *Medical Education in the United Stated and Canada* (Princeton, NJ: Carnegie Foundation for the Advancement of Teaching, 1910).

59 http://jpands.org/vol8no2/hiattext.pdf

offer the only doctorate with a consistent curriculum. If you have a PhD in math, you may not have taken the same courses as you would have at another university. Doctors study the same curriculum no matter where they are. That's a good thing, but it was only as a result of a report that revealed terrible problems in the medical field.

At least one of those controversies from the Flexner Report still rings true: too few doctors. Consider again the VHA, which has a shortfall of more than 45,000 clinical positions. Another unanticipated result of the reforms of the early twentieth century that led to raising the quality and profile of medical doctors was that the rest of us began to put doctors on a pedestal. Sometimes it almost seems like they're unapproachable. That's why it's important to humanize doctors. It makes a tremendous difference when you're comfortable having a dialogue with your doctor. If you're going to be active in your own care, you need the doctor to be your trusted consultant, so you can solve problems together.

The Flexner Report ushered in a period of tremendous growth for the healthcare industry, and it's time again for us to take a similar leap forward.

MOVING TO A MORE COLLABORATIVE, COOPERATIVE MODEL

The chronic nature of much of the population's health

problems requires coordination and management. Integrated delivery models are coming, and compensation methods are beginning to leverage the private sector so that market efficiencies can be realized in delivering care. Those are some of the bright spots on the horizon. Yet, the slow evolution to the more appropriate chronic-care model is a problem.

Healthcare is hard. That's something we must face. It's hard enough just in terms of what you have to do to improve your own health. Eating right and exercising, keeping a good mindset, sleeping enough—those are hard to achieve. Add to that the fundamental difficulty with a system that's disjointed, confusing, and complicated and we start to see how hard this really is. That's why we have this book, so that before your time comes, if it hasn't already, you can be prepared.

Again, it's a team sport, and you have to play your role. That's not an order, just a fact. You've got an obligation. You might escape from disease, but you won't escape the system. You may not get cancer, but you're going to deal with our healthcare system at some point, whether you like it or not. That's why understanding the system is so important. Only through our actions, based on our satisfaction or dissatisfaction, is the system going to change.

This chapter has outlined many of the problems in the

healthcare system itself. The chapters in Part II focus on things you can do immediately to impact your health. Such things don't require repealing or replacing the Affordable Care Act. They don't require Democrats and Republicans to get along. They don't require the president to change anything. They are things you can control, much of which is related to nutrition, movement, and mindset.

PART II

FIGHTING THE GOOD FIGHT: ARMING YOURSELF

CHAPTER 4

NUTRITION: YOU ARE WHAT YOU EAT

NEED-TO-KNOW NUGGETS

- Improving your nutrition is the single most important thing you can do to influence your health.
- Epigenetics: Your environment, including nutrition, influences how your DNA expresses itself.
- Microbiome: You are what you eat—no, really!

Part II is about the things that you can control in order to arm yourself for the healthcare battle: nutrition (Chapter 4), movement (Chapter 5), and mindset (Chapter 6). Food is more than we think it is. We know it fuels our body and that it can be good or bad for us. It's more than just the raw materials your body needs to function. Food, and even the smell of food, becomes the instruction manual that your body uses to make its own decisions. Each bite you take is its own little message.

When you eat food, you're getting not only the energy and nutrients, like vitamins and minerals that you need, you're getting a set of signals and instructions for everything that makes up your body. Your cells talk to each other, or communicate with each other, through a process called cell signaling. Armed with this knowledge, you can prioritize nutrition as a way to protect and improve your health.

Most people think that the only thing living in their body is their body. Wrong. There are a mind-boggling number of bacteria and other microorganisms living in your body, called the human microbiome. Few people realize just what a huge part of you this is. Recent estimates say there are just as many bacteria in your body as there are your own cells, and some estimates are that there are ten times as many. Think about that: numerically speaking, there are more of these other living things in your body than there is of you!

Everybody knows we've all got DNA in our cells, which contains instructions for creating you as a human being. But you've also got another set of DNA residing in the bacteria living in your gut. These bacteria that live in your body also get instructions from the food you eat, and those bacteria impact how your own DNA expresses itself.[60]

60 https://ghr.nlm.nih.gov/primer/howgeneswork/geneonoff

Let's think about how this relates to aging. I want to share an analogy I call "the hill versus the cliff." When people say someone is "over the hill," they're talking about hitting a downtrend in terms of age and vitality. They've passed the midpoint. Usually people say this starts happening at forty or fifty, and it has a negative connotation, but I think we need to start viewing it differently. Let's say I'm skiing or mountain biking. When I go over the hill, it's *fun*. In fact, it's the best part. At least, it can be. It's up to you, because you're the one who builds the hill.

When you're young and developing your patterns of what you eat and how you behave, that's you building your hill. You want that hill to be fun to go down when you reach it in the later stages of your life. But if you're not careful, you might not be building a hill at all. You might be building a cliff.

Hippocrates, the Classical Greek physician known as the father of modern medicine, said, "Let food be thy medicine and medicine be thy food." And he had it right. Probably the single most important thing you can do is to eat the right food and educate yourself about it.

Food is chemical energy—fuel for your body. The quality of fuel you put in your body matters. You don't put regular unleaded gas in a high-performance race car, for example. If you did, you would get a lot of by-products that impact the engine system. The fuel doesn't burn right, and it creates residue. You have too much carbon where it doesn't belong, and it impacts how things run. You don't get the optimum performance out of the vehicle.

The same goes for your body. If you put junk into it, it's going to slow down and not perform as well as it would if you put high-quality nutrients into it. The fuel matters, and it matters more than you might think, because nutrition to the body is exponentially more complex than fuel is to a vehicle.

Think of your body as a supercomputer and food as both the electricity and software. Better yet, your body is a construction site using nutrition as both the power and raw materials to build new cells. We can all understand the consequences of poor construction.

No matter how you look at it, nutrition is the single best thing that you can do to help yourself be healthier. It's a powerful weapon on the healthcare battlefield. But there are hazards.

Take, for example, potato chips, and the process to create them.

Potato chips are not designed to be nutritious food. They're designed so that you eat more and more of them and keep buying them. The companies who make potato chips have discovered how to make them not as nutritious as possible, but as delicious as possible.

Your tongue is a fairly simple sensor. It detects salt, sugar, and bitterness. Therefore, it's easy to trick it into thinking that it's getting something great, and that it needs more. In 2013, *The New York Times Magazine* published an article titled "The Extraordinary Science of Addictive Junk Food."

According to the article, "Frito-Lay had a formidable research complex near Dallas, where nearly 500 chemists, psychologists and technicians conducted research that cost up to $30 million a year, and the science corps focused intense amounts of resources on questions of crunch, mouth feel and aroma for each of these items. Their tools included a $40,000 device that simulated a chewing mouth to test and perfect the chips, discovering things like the perfect break point: people like a chip that snaps with about four pounds of pressure per square inch."[61]

Now, it's not that I don't appreciate all the work they put into my snacking pleasure. In fact, it's a great example of how the private sector can innovate to satisfy customers. The healthcare industry could learn a thing or two.

---

61 http://www.nytimes.com/2013/02/24/magazine/the-extraordinary-science-of-junk-food.html

Unfortunately, as great as snacking can occasionally be, it's also a land mine on the healthcare battlefield. Clearly, we're outgunned here. It's a chink in our armor unless we understand what we're eating and how it affects us. Otherwise our bodies are going to believe the enemy.

GENETICS AND EPIGENETICS

We learned in school you've got twenty-three pairs of chromosomes, half of which you inherit from your mother, half from your father. These tell our body what to do, literally sending messages to make the proteins and molecules we need to develop and grow. Simplistically, you know you got your blue eyes and blond hair or brown eyes and brown hair from the combination of your parents' genes. That's what we think of when we think of DNA, but that's only a small part of its role.

The genes of DNA can be switched on or switched off.[62] Whether a gene expresses itself, that is, whether it gets turned on or off, is impacted by your environment and your mindset. The things you choose to do, where you live—and what you eat—all impact what's expressed.

This brings us to the emerging field of epigenetics, which is concerned with how the environment influences what's expressed by our DNA. DNA loads the gun, but environ-

---

62 https://ghr.nlm.nih.gov/primer/howgeneswork/geneonoff

ment pulls the trigger. The environment causes your DNA to behave differently. Epigenetics is the study of how the environment affects the expression of genes. The word *epigenetics* literally means above genetics or in addition to genetics.[63]

Examples of this are being found everywhere. There are studies suggesting that people born after a particular famine have a higher likelihood of developing cancer. You may have a gene that leads to a certain type of cancer, for example, but whether that gene gets turned on or off depends in part on what you eat and what the rest of your environment is like. Or there may be a mother who has some sort of stressful episode while pregnant, and then later in life the baby develops some complications. It's possible the mother's traumatic event may have caused certain genes of hers to be expressed and others to be switched off.

Food is part of your environment. Changes in what food you choose to put in your body can cause changes to this master controller of gene expression. In this way, the old adage is true: you literally are what you eat.

---

63 https://www.whatisepigenetics.com/what-is-epigenetics/

HOW EPIGENETIC MECHANISMS CAN AFFECT HEALTH

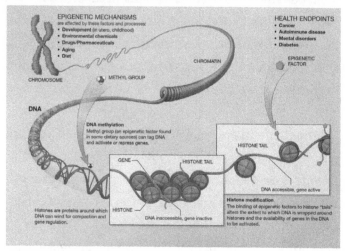

"A Scientific Illustration of How Epigenetic Mechanisms Can Affect Health" illustration courtesy of the National Institutes of Health.[64]

THE MICROBIOME AND ITS ROLE IN NUTRITION

When you're born, you immediately start picking up bacteria from the environment, including your mother's body. These bacteria start colonizing you, eventually becoming a part of you in a symbiotic relationship. One thing the bacteria do is work with the food you eat to give your body instructions (which I'll get to in a minute), as well as use the nutrition. The bacteria that live in your gut play a key part in that. Which parts of your DNA express themselves and which don't are influenced by that. The microbiome and epigenetics, I believe, are the mechanics of how evolution ultimately works.

---

64 "A Scientific Illustration of How Epigenetic Mechanisms Can Affect Health," National Institutes of Health. https://commonfund.nih.gov/epigenomics/figure

The microbiome does incredibly powerful things for you. It teaches your body how to recognize dangerous invaders. It tells your immune system when and how to attack. It generates anti-inflammatory compounds. One groundbreaking theory is that if you can understand a person's individual microbiome, then you can use that to fight disease. In 2008, the National Institutes of Health launched the Human Microbiome Project[65] to promote research into the human microbiome and explore its role in human health and disease. What they found was incredible: "The more we learn about the human microbiome—the trillions of single-celled organisms that colonize our skin, nose, digestive system...—the more we realize that the microscopic critters that live on us and in us may be as important to our health as our body cells."[66]

For example, most people know that eating yogurt is good for them. It's good because yogurt is *probiotic*, meaning it has beneficial live bacteria that colonize inside you and go on living inside you. Surprisingly, your yogurt bacteria need to eat something too, which is fiber. So, if you have some yogurt before bed, try eating something high in fiber, a *prebiotic* (what probiotics eat), to feed the new bacteria. You've probably heard the expression "eating for two," but what we are really eating for is more like 2 trillion!

---

65 https://www.ncbi.nlm.nih.gov/pmc/articles/PMC2792171/

66 https://www.health.harvard.edu/press_releases/
    making-peace-with-your-germs-from-the-february-2016-harvard-womens-health-watch

A somewhat radical new approach to making sure people have the right kinds of germs in their intestines are fecal transplants.[67] If you're wondering if you are correct in assuming what that is, you're probably right. Sometimes antibiotics kill the good bacteria, allowing bad bacteria to overpopulate. The solution is to introduce more of the good bacteria. Fecal transplants involve literally taking one person's poop and putting it into another person. There's obviously a detailed procedure for this, but that's the long and the short of it—someone else's poop becomes your poop, and you reap the microbial rewards. Gross? Maybe. Important? Incredibly so.

Epigenetics and the human microbiome are still emerging fields of study and are therefore not yet widely accepted and discussed. It takes time for new ideas and technologies to be widely adopted, a topic I focus on more in Chapter 8. Still, we have them, and they are tools that point toward a future where medicine harnesses the powers already residing in the body to help it protect itself. In other words, you're already armed to fight the enemy, even if you don't realize it.

MACRONUTRIENTS AND MICRONUTRIENTS

Your body has different dietary needs. Very generally

---

67   https://www.hopkinsmedicine.org/gastroenterology_hepatology/clinical_services/advanced_
    endoscopy/fecal_transplantation.html

speaking, you need to consume the right macronutrients and micronutrients. Macronutrients are the things you need in larger quantities—your carbohydrates, proteins, and fats.

Micronutrients are your vitamins and minerals. A vitamin, simply put, is an organic substance that you need to live. Organic substances come from plants or animals. A mineral is nonorganic, but it's something that still occurs in nature. They both fall under the category of micronutrients because you need such small amounts of them. However, despite being needed in such small quantities, they are vital to your health.

RECOMMENDED DAILY, I MEAN DIETARY, ALLOWANCE

I was talking to my friend and neighbor, Morrow, who is a geneticist, psychologist, and MD. He was telling me that, given my size and lifestyle, I need to take a lot of B complex vitamins. Now, if I take 100 percent of something, that seems like the right amount. But here was a person I trust telling me to take 2,000 percent of the recommended dietary allowance (RDA) of B complex vitamins.[68] I set out to try to understand how this could be.

We've all heard of the RDA—what we've come to think of

---

68 http://science.sciencemag.org/content/sci/101/2621/285.full.
    pdf?ijkey=6df498329709e2fa06e9d1a1a5792da29e7d70a9&keytype2=tf_ipsecsha

as the recommended daily allowance of different nutrients. However, it actually stands for the recommended *dietary* allowance.

The RDA was established in 1941 during World War II. The health of the population in the wake of the Great Depression and wartime rationing was of interest to national security.[69] Leaders were worried about failing to meet the nutritional needs of the population. Vitamin deficiencies were causing problems, healthy workers still needed the energy to do their jobs, and leaders didn't want people getting sick. So, the US government sought to establish what the population needed in terms of nutrition. Their guidelines were a set of allowances for energy and eight nutrients. It was a standard that would be used for nutrition recommendation for the armed forces, civilians, and overseas populations who might need food relief.

The Food and Nutrition Board kept revising the RDA every five to ten years. In the early fifties, the Department of Agriculture and Nutrition made a new guideline of its own and included the food groups with each nutrient.

It's important to remember that this was initially developed during a time of war. We may not think of food rationing in World War II, but during the war, everything was rationed. The recommended dietary allowance, there-

---

69 https://www.agriculture.senate.gov/imo/media/doc/Testimony_Hawley.pdf

fore, is not a guideline for living your healthiest. In fact, it actually represents the *minimum* amount that people need so that 97.5 percent of the population don't get sick. So, when you read that you need "100 percent" of a certain vitamin, for example, that's 100 percent of the minimum. It's not the ideal amount—it's just enough that you don't fall ill from some disease, because you *will* get sick if you don't get enough of these nutrients. For example, a lack of iron can cause anemia, but introducing some shellfish or kidney beans can largely solve that problem.

People know the RDA mainly through food labels. When a label says 100 percent, you probably think that sounds like enough. After all, if you get 100 percent in school, you're doing as well as you can do! But really, it's not enough. In fact, even at that amount, 2.5 percent of the population are going to get sick. The RDA is also usually based on a 2,000- to 2,500-calorie diet and, nowadays, most people don't need that many calories for the lifestyle that they lead.[70]

THE ABCs & Ds OF NUTRITION (FAT OR FICTION)

If you ask your doctor if you need supplements, your doctor is likely to say no, if you eat right, you're okay. But what does *eating right* mean? It's not always so simple. You need the right kinds of vitamins, but you also need

---

70 https://www.fda.gov/Food/LabelingNutrition/ucm274593.htm

them in the right amount for you. To get the vitamins you need just from your food, you'll be eating a ton of fruits and vegetables—and even then, you might not be getting enough of everything. Take B vitamins, for example. Your body doesn't make them. They have to be consumed and are found in different meats and some vegetables. Now, B vitamins are water-soluble, meaning that if you have too many, they just get washed away with water. But that's not true of all vitamins.

Vitamin D, for example, is very different. Your body needs it just like it needs B vitamins, but they work very differently. Your body, to start, actually makes vitamin D. Many of us know this—when we get enough sun, we know our body is making vitamin D. Like vitamin B, it's possible to have too much, but unlike vitamin B, vitamin D is fat-soluble. That means it doesn't just wash away, and that can be trouble.

The native peoples of the Arctic have never shied away from cooking up some polar bear stew, but they've long known to avoid eating the livers of various arctic creatures. Western explorers, however, learned the hard way. As early as 1596, explorers returned to Europe with accounts of horrible illnesses resulting from the consumption of polar bear liver.[71] The polar bear's liver, much like those of arctic seals and huskies, contains extremely high levels of retinol (the form of vitamin A found in members of the animal kingdom).[72]

There are consequences if you don't educate yourself about nutrition. For example, there's confusion over "healthy fats." I was talking to somebody today who is quite intelligent, but she was surprised when I told her that salmon contains healthy fat. You want to get enough of those kinds of fats. They help your body and brain work. I saw a TV show in which a guy in London ate a traditional, unhealthy breakfast of bangers and mash. An hour or so later, he drew his blood and ran it through a centrifuge. It showed fat congealing from the sausage he had eaten. As obvious as it may seem, I don't think people understand that when you put food in your body, it goes into your bloodstream before it is burned for energy or stored for future use.

If you're putting good fat like that from salmon in you,

---

71 https://animals.howstuffworks.com/mammals/eat-polar-bear-liver.htm

72 https://animals.howstuffworks.com/mammals/eat-polar-bear-liver.htm

then it's doing good work in your body. It's like a higher grade of oil in an engine. Now, this is just an illustration, but please consider a cup of milk. If you pour milk into a cup and then pour it out, you'll see a white film on the inside of the glass. When dealing with fat, that same film would be found in your arteries and veins. You want good stuff, like the fat from that salmon, to be there as residue, not bad stuff. When you eat trans fats, where scientists have gone out of their way to jam an extra hydrogen molecule[73] into something that's been superheated to produce something tasty that doesn't exist in nature, your body doesn't know what to do with that. That's why it's illegal now to put trans fats in food.[74] Many things we put in our bodies help cause cancer. The knowledge of what they are and how they impact your body is very powerful.

Vitamins and minerals work in concert. Many of us know that if you're missing a particular mineral or vitamin, you'll get a particular illness. As we mentioned, a lack of iron can lead to anemia. What isn't as widely known is how nutrients work together. For example, vitamin C can help you absorb iron-rich foods, but it can also block your absorption of copper. Vitamin D can help you get calcium out of food instead of taking it from your bones, but too much can be harmful by making your blood cal-

---

73 https://www.fda.gov/Food/PopularTopics/ucm292278.htm

74 https://www.fda.gov/Food/IngredientsPackagingLabeling/FoodAdditivesIngredients/
    ucm449162.htm

cium too high. There's a very complex relationship among nutrients that only a nutritionist would fully appreciate. But the fact remains that if a poor diet can make you sick, an ideal diet can make you well. That's a function of how nutrients work together with your body, and with all the things like bacteria living in and on you (yes, I know, ew).

How do you educate yourself, though? How can you learn more about this, especially if your own doctor is not a nutritionist? The good news is, there's a lot of great information out there. I recommend the National Institutes of Health website (www.nih.gov), which is free to access and can really help you understand what various vitamins and minerals do.

BEWARE THE DOUBLE-EDGED SWORD

Of course, you can have too much of a good thing. By now you've probably heard that drinking a glass of red wine every day or every other day is good for your heart.[75] That doesn't mean drinking ten glasses would be better. This kind of double-edged sword is illustrated by a J-shaped curve. The little curl at the bottom of a capital J starts by going down. Having one glass of wine, for example (here, down is good). Then there's a part where you bend around the curve (maybe this is three glasses) and it starts going up and up and up. As you get to the top of the J, after ten glasses of wine, you're much worse off.

---

75   https://www.consumerreports.org/wine/health-benefits-of-wine/

What matters is what you do on a regular basis. It's not your birthday celebration on a Saturday night you should be thinking about. It's your regular routine—what you're normally doing, not what you occasionally do—that has a cumulative effect. A dermatologist will tell you that skin cancer is cumulative and that all your lifetime exposure over the years adds up. On the other hand, another doctor will tell you that if you don't get enough vitamin D, which is made by your skin when it's exposed to sunlight, you're at risk of colon cancer and, for women, breast cancer. Which doctor should you believe?

You should believe both. This, too, is a J-shaped curve. A little sun is necessary, but too much is detrimental. People naturally want simple answers to complex questions, and when they don't get those answers, they tend to get overwhelmed and frustrated. There is a lot of conflicting information out there. Hopefully, understanding the dynamics of the J-shaped curve can help put things into context.

ANTIOXIDANTS AND FREE RADICALS

Free radicals, or oxidants, are unstable molecules that can damage DNA, and we all need substances called antioxidants in our food to handle them. Antioxidants neutralize unstable molecules, so they can't harm our cells. I've been talking about how genes in DNA express themselves or not, and the relationship between nutrition, your environment, your epigenetics, and the bacteria in your body that help make up your microbiome. The way these things work together makes up a good part of your health.

The processes your body goes through, the things you do, the injuries you may suffer—in other words, normal functions of living life—promote free radicals, which have to be neutralized, and antioxidants as part of nutrition are what neutralizes them. Whether it's vitamin E, making sure you're getting plenty of fruits and vegetables, or (in my case) a glass of red wine at night, we all need to take in antioxidants to neutralize free radicals.

Foods rich in antioxidants neutralize free radicals by giving up some of their own electrons. Vitamins C and E, for example, make that sacrifice. They have what amounts to an off switch for free radicals.

Free radical: an atom or molecule that bears an unpaired electron and is extremely reactive, capable of engaging in rapid chain reactions that destabilize other molecules and generate many more free radicals. In the body, free radicals are deactivated by antioxidants, uric acid, and certain enzyme activities. In animal tissues, free radicals can damage cells and are believed to accelerate the progression of cancer, cardiovascular disease, and age-related diseases.[76]

I travel the world educating myself on health. When I see a speaker, I always make a point to talk to them afterward and ask the same question: what's the most important thing people can do for their health? No matter where I go, no matter what country I'm in, they usually say the same thing: nutrition. You simply must take your nutrition seriously.

Once you understand that, you also need to understand that nutrition alone won't get you where you need to be. You still have to move, and that's what we'll discuss in the next chapter.

---

76 http://www.dictionary.com/browse/free-radical?s=t

CHAPTER 5

MOVEMENT: DON'T GUM UP THE WORKS

NEED-TO-KNOW NUGGETS

- Your body is an advanced machine.
- Use it or lose it.
- Mitochondria jump-start natural energy.

In the military, I learned that if you take care of your body, your body will take care of you. I also learned you can help take care of someone else. At Fort Bragg, I was doing a particular exercise and some guy I didn't know saw what I was doing and helped me with my technique. He gave me a photocopy of a great strength-and-conditioning program. I benefited from that—just one person being helpful to another person. That attitude is one of my favorite things about the military, but it's also something you can find on your own.

Your body is built to move. If you don't move, as you'll learn in this chapter, your body can't take care of the cells that make it up. You're vulnerable to attack. Just like a vehicle that sits somewhere unused, without movement your body will eventually seize up. Think about something simple like how a lawnmower works. When I was a kid, we would go to Cleveland for the summer. Before leaving, we would drain the gas out of the lawnmower because we knew that if it sat unused like that for several months, it would gum up. The engine wouldn't work right by the time we started it up again.

Notice that I call it *movement*, not *exercise*. Exercise is movement, to be sure, but some people think if they're doing a little weight routine a couple times a week that they're getting enough exercise. But that's not all your body needs. What you need is to move and be active. My friend keeps up a golf course. He's up early and walks the golf course all day; that would certainly be adequate movement. Don't get me wrong—strength conditioning and flexibility are incredibly important, and in fact become even more important over time because you tend to lose muscle mass and flexibility as you get older, and you have to actively counter that. But you don't have to do that all at once. A really good start is simply walking 10,000 steps a day. If you do that, you're doing more than most people are.

Both the term and the specific exercise method were developed by Dr. Kenneth H. Cooper, an exercise physiologist, and Col. Pauline Potts, a physical therapist, both of the United States Air Force. Dr. Cooper, an avowed exercise enthusiast, was personally and professionally puzzled about why some people with excellent muscular strength were still prone to poor performance at tasks such as long-distance running, swimming, and bicycling. He began measuring systematic human performance using a bicycle ergometer and began measuring sustained performance in terms of a person's ability to use oxygen.

In 1968, he published *Aerobics*, which included exercise programs using running, walking, swimming and bicycling. The book came at a time when increasing weakness and inactivity in the general population was causing a perceived need for increased exercise.[77]

MOVEMENT AND THE CIRCULATORY SYSTEM

Movement helps *perfusion*, which is how blood is delivered to bodily tissue.[78] In other words, movement helps the circulatory system get the nutrients to the cells that need them. Think about your body at the cellular level. In a very real way, movement allows the body to work

---

77   Cooper, Kenneth H. (January 1969) [1968]. Aerobics. 14490 (revised ed.). Bantam Books. ISBN 978-0-553-14490-1. Lay summary (2007-12-28).

78   https://www.ncbi.nlm.nih.gov/pmc/articles/PMC2894463/

and stops the body from shutting down. The body is an efficient machine. If you're not using it, it's going to turn off. Movement and flexibility directly impact your overall well-being.

Again, in life, you create your own hill. What you do is cumulative in terms of conditioning, flexibility, and injury. When you're young, your body does a better job of taking care of itself. Movement can give you great things like more strength and better endurance on top of simply staying healthy. But at some point, your body starts to deteriorate, and in time you have to work hard just to maintain your health. If you've built a nice hill, then as you get older and lose some strength, you've defended yourself. You've built a nice hill to roll down. It's a more fun, easier ride. Movement is a big part of maintaining your hill.

We need to think about movement and exercise in the context of keeping the machine running. Weight matters, but we're talking about the long-term big picture here. Your weight, after all, is going to be a by-product of your overall activity. Nutritionists can help you design a good diet, which was the topic of Chapter 4. And just like nutrition, it's much more complicated than it sounds. Just as there is a relationship between the types and amounts of foods you eat, there is also a relationship between activity, strength conditioning, and flexibility. And just like your diet, you will need to find a movement regimen that is right for you.

Personally, I like the Master Fitness Trainer Course (MFTC) I learned in the service.[79] There are a wide range of programs to choose from. Recent studies highlight the merits of yoga, tai chi, and Pilates, which all offer great blends of movement, flexibility, breathing, and strength training. Remember, movement helps your circulatory system get nutrients to where they need to be, and it's how the system removes things that should not be there anymore. Your body is an amazing engine. It converts chemical energy from nutrients. It removes the by-products, some of which can be toxic. It's a self-correcting organism. But it can only conduct its activities through movement.

MITOCHONDRIA: THE CELL'S POWER PLANT

Each of your cells has its own generator, called *mitochondria*.[80] Digesting your food is just the beginning of the whole process. The mitochondria are the real engines in your body. They break down the nutrients you consume into energy-rich molecules. When you want your muscles to move or your heart to beat, that all happens through the mitochondria. You need loads of mitochondria in

79 https://www.army.mil/standto/archive_2014-08-25

80 https://ghr.nlm.nih.gov/primer/basics/mtdna

your muscles to do this work, and where the heavy work is happening is where you need the mitochondria. In other words, you have control over the mitochondria in your cells in different parts of your body. If you put high demands on the cell, it can make more mitochondria. When you think about different muscles in your body—take, for example, your heart—you can see just how important it is to work those muscles.

One interesting fact about mitochondria is that billions of years ago, they were their own separate beings.[81] They even have a small amount of their own DNA, called mitochondrial DNA (mDNA). Some sort of symbiosis happened long ago, where the mitochondria became part of the cells of other creatures. So, rather like the human microbiome discussed in Chapter 4, here we have another tiny part of you that isn't, or once wasn't, human.

All your cells except red blood cells, hair, and nails, have mitochondria. A typical cell might have 1,000 or more mitochondria.[82] One person might have one trillion mitochondria, and another person might have two trillion. That largely depends on their activity level. If you've lived a sedentary lifestyle, you can bring more mitochondria

---

81 http://www.sciencemag.org/news/2016/02/
    why-do-our-cells-power-plants-have-their-own-dna

82 http://bscb.org/learning-resources/softcell-e-learning/
    mitochondrion-much-more-than-an-energy-converter/

online. Think of rolling a large, heavy tire. It can be hard to get it rolling at first, but once you get it moving, it's easier to keep it moving. And when you get your tire—or, rather, your body—moving, you're giving your mitochondria the motivation they need to turn back on.

Why does this matter? Mitochondria make energy. The more you have, the more energy you have. How you feel when you wake up in the morning is at least in part a function of the number of mitochondria you have. Think of them like an army. The more you have, the better your defenses are.

SEDENTARY VERSUS ACTIVE MITOCHONDRIA ILLUSTRATION

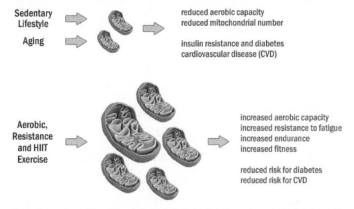

Sedentary Lifestyle

Aging

reduced aerobic capacity
reduced mitochondrial number

insulin resistance and diabetes
cardiovascular disease (CVD)

Aerobic, Resistance and HIIT Exercise

increased aerobic capacity
increased resistance to fatigue
increased endurance
increased fitness

reduced risk for diabetes
reduced risk for CVD

Illustration courtesy of Cyrus Khambatta, PhD, Mastering Diabetes, www.masteringdiabetes.org[83]

83   Cyrus Khambatta, "Mastering Diabetes." www.masteringdiabetes.org

The natural cycle is for cells to eventually die off. They have a limited lifespan, and a natural tendency to slow down. Cells replicate fifty to seventy times before you die.[84] Each time they replicate, errors can creep in. Think about the old copy machines: when you make a copy of a copy of a copy, the original image gets lost. As DNA replicates, maybe five bits fall out here, twenty bits fall out there. You can counter that tendency with movement and activity, because the body will step up to the demands you place on it. Movement can override the master controller. If you keep your muscles strong and keep flexible by maintaining your range of motion and continuing to move, your body is going to behave differently than that of someone who doesn't do those things. You'll have more energy. Your body is better armed to defend itself.

Prevention is better than cure. Let's look at shoulder injuries, for example, which are common.[85] Your shoulders are an area you may not normally worry about in your exercise routines, but it's important to know that you can work the muscles that keep your shoulders intact. If you don't move those muscles, you risk injury. And if you'd been doing the exercises to begin with, you probably wouldn't have gotten injured in the first place.

---

84 https://www.yourgenome.org/facts/what-is-a-telomere

85 https://www.news-medical.net/news/20101001/Shoulder-pain-costs-American-health-system-247-billion.aspx

I can tell you from my own personal experience that pre-habilitation is a lot better than rehabilitation.

Twenty five out of 1,000 visits to the family doctor are related to shoulder pain, which is also the cause of 13% of sick leaves and costs the American health system $7 billion annually. Shoulder pain is more prevalent in the elderly and in women (25%), and is a contributor to depression and self-perception of poor health.[86]

Movement is the only way of nailing down this part of preventative health, from areas of your body as large as your shoulders, all the way down to your cells. If you're a couch potato who eats salads and takes supplements, your cells simply won't be getting what they need. Your mitochondria and your body will start to slow down. Remember, your body is efficient—it will simply start to turn off because the machine won't work the way it was designed to work.

---

86 https://www.futuremedicine.com/doi/abs/10.2217/ahe.09.48

In a 2014 study published in Epigenetics, scientists at the Karo-
linska Institute in Sweden asked 23 men and women to bicycle
using only one leg for 45 minutes, four times a week over
three months. In comparing muscle biopsies before and after
the experiment, scientists found that, in the exercised muscle,
new patterns had developed on genes associated with insulin
response, inflammation, and energy metabolism.

TELOMERES—TELL YOUR YEARS

TELOMERES AT THE END OF OUR CHROMOSOMES

Chromosome

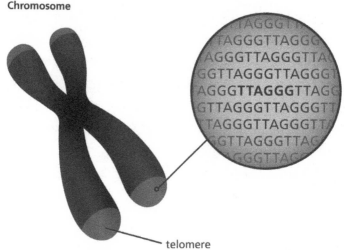

telomere

Illustration showing the position of telomeres at the end of our chromosomes courtesy of
yourgenome.org[87]

One way to try to measure the aging process is thought
to involve the telomere.[88] Telomeres are sort of like a

---

87   yourgenome.org, https://www.yourgenome.org/facts/what-is-a-telomere

88   https://www.yourgenome.org/facts/what-is-a-telomere

wrapper in your DNA that keeps the chromosomes in place. Think about a shoelace. On the end of a shoelace, you've got that little plastic tip that allows it to go through the grommet or eyelet of the shoe. Eventually, that plastic tip starts to crack and peel away, and pretty soon you have the frayed end of a shoelace, which can be hard to use. Similarly, your DNA has a telomere wrapper to keep the chromosomes in place, but the wrapper doesn't last forever. As the end of the telomere starts to fray and get shorter, that seems to be an indicator of where you are in terms of life span. Each time your cells replicate, you actually lose a couple of chromosomes. Over time, depending on how many you lose in each replication, the result is the aging process. Again, think of it like a photocopying machine making fuzzier and fuzzier copies. If all your cells replicated perfectly, every time, we wouldn't age—or die. We can't live forever, but we definitely have control over how long those protective wrappers, telomeres, stay in good shape. If you practice the advice in this book, especially incorporating movement, your telomeres will stay in better shape, for longer.

As I've said throughout this book, you are in charge of your health and, as you can now see, you can affect the process. Your lifestyle and your environment are big determinants in your health. Some estimates say that you can add five to seven years to your life by taking charge of your body and how it functions. But as we've also seen, life spans, depending on location (environment) can vary by up to twenty years![89] There is a twenty-year variance in the United States alone. In Virginia, there is a seventeen-year difference in average life spans between areas near Washington, DC, versus rural areas of the state—that's a tremendous difference within one state. There's an even more dramatic example. In Texas, research shows the adjusted mortality rate for patients enrolled in a Medicare Advantage plan, with a particular provider group, was consistently and considerably lower compared with the Texas senior population as a whole.[90] There are of course lots of variables that can be at play—but how you take care of yourself (which includes the primary-care doctor you select) is certainly one of them.

A final thought on prolonging the aging process is to think about becoming the new you. If your cells really do replicate fifty to seventy times over an average life span of over seventy-nine years, that means they are replicating every year or so. That means, in theory, if you eat right, embrace an active lifestyle, and keep a positive mindset, you can technically recreate yourself at the cellular level in just over a year. Like I said in the last chapter, you are what you eat, literally.

---

89 http://www.npr.org/sections/health-shots/2017/05/08/527103885/
life-expectancy-can-vary-by-20-years-depending-on-where-you-live

90 WellMed Medical Group, "Research Shows WellMed Seniors Living Longer Than 65+
Population in Texas," (press statement, 2011).

The SENS Research Foundation, co-founded by Aubrey de Grey[91], is trying to help people live longer, healthier lives by viewing aging as a disease.

The SENS Research Foundation is focused on a damage-repair approach to treating the diseases of aging. This approach has the potential to positively affect the human condition by giving people interventions and treatments that yield more years of healthy, productive life.[92]

YOUR BODY'S DEFENSIVE AND OFFENSIVE CAPABILITIES

The circulatory system involves your blood and the nutrients and waste it carries to and from your cells. As a child, we all learn about how blood flows through veins and the arteries throughout your body. What we don't all learn about is the lymphatic system, which is closely associated to the circulatory system, but something entirely different.[93]

The lymphatic system is similarly designed for transportation, but it's not about oxygen and nutrients. The lymphatic system carries lymph fluid, which is like the cleanup crew for your body. We're mostly made of water

91 https://www.ted.com/speakers/aubrey_de_grey

92 http://www.sens.org/sites/srf.org/files/reports/SENS%20Research%20Foundation%20Annual%20Report%202016.pdf

93 https://www2.estrellamountain.edu/faculty/farabee/biobk/BioBookIMMUN.html

and other fluids.[94] Those fluids are usually contained in the cells, but cell fluid often seeps out, and this intercellular fluid starts to accumulate. You may have flown in an airplane and noticed your ankles swelling up. That's because you didn't move, so your lymph system didn't work. Once you landed and stood up and walked, the swelling went down. The lymphatic system gathers up these fluids that are left lying around and puts them back into your bloodstream, sending them back to the heart.

Normally, people only think about their lymph nodes when they're sick. We know that when cancer reaches them, it's bad news. The doctor feels your throat or under your arms or inside your thigh, and that's the extent of how we think of lymph nodes. Your lymph nodes are actually part of your immune system, part of how you defend yourself. The lymph nodes make some of the white blood cells that kill pathogens. That means they're involved in more than just defense—they provide offense. The lymphatic system fuels the immune system, which is constantly patrolling your body, and if it finds an invader, it attacks the invader and digests it. It makes it go away.

---

94 http://www.allaboutwater.org/water-facts.html

YOUR BODY'S OFFENSIVE CAPABILITY

PHAGOCYTOSIS

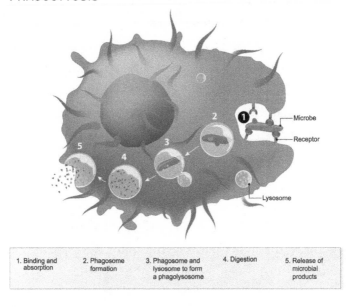

1. Binding and absorption	2. Phagosome formation	3. Phagosome and lysosome to form a phagolysosome	4. Digestion	5. Release of microbial products

The lymphatic system is not one that you hear much about. But it's there, moving fluid around your body—and it only moves because *you* move. Unlike your circulatory system, it doesn't have a heart to pump the fluid, just your muscles. Fighting off disease, therefore, literally depends on movement. You balance the nutrition you take in with engaging in enough movement, and you dramatically improve your odds, health-wise.

The theme of this book is that health is a battlefield, and that's never more true than when talking about the immune system. The military defends in layers. Antiterrorism is one of those layers. Counterterrorism is another layer; it's about taking the fight to the enemy. Counterterrorism is like the white blood cells going out and taking down pathogens. In the military, I worked on teams that focused on the leadership of the bad guys around the world, the nefarious people who wanted to hurt our country and our citizens. We went out and actively found that leadership and dealt with them. You can make your body do the same thing by actively enabling your body's defensive and offensive abilities. And you do that by taking control of your nutrition and your movement.

Equally as important, yet less understood than nutrition and movement, is mindset. And that's the topic of the next chapter.

CHAPTER 6

MINDSET: YOU CAN WORRY YOURSELF SICK

NEED-TO-KNOW NUGGETS

- Mindset matters.
- You can worry yourself sick.
- You can hack happiness.

Just as we can prepare ourselves physically through nutrition and movement, we can prepare mentally, emotionally, and psychologically through mindset, and that's just as important. We are empowered by our intelligence to make certain choices that are denied to other creatures. When the sun shines, the flower opens. When you get too close to a snake, it bites. Not much thought goes into those actions. With humans, between the stimulus and the response, there's often a choice. The fact is that we do have the ability to choose, and that is part of what makes us different from other species. This makes things complicated, because our choices are impacted by filters based on genetics, upbringing, and our current situation. That means that two people could see the same thing and interpret it in two different ways.

That's part of what I mean by mindset. You have the power to choose. You can make a choice to positively impact and protect yourself and your well-being. We've talked about nutrition and movement as building blocks for improving health and fighting disease. The third one, mindset, is about using that unique human ability to choose, and the power associated with those choices.

THE POWER OF THE CONTRAPOSITIVE

A foundational concept of this chapter is the idea of the contrapositive.[95] Simply stated, it means that the opposite of something is true: the opposite of up is down; the opposite of right is wrong; the opposite of good is bad; the opposite of sick is healthy. And because of this, I believe if you can "worry yourself sick," you can "will yourself well."

If you have a negative mindset, there are real-life con-

---

95 http://www.mathwords.com/c/contrapositive.htm

sequences. You've heard expressions like "worried sick" and "died of a broken heart." These are real things. Stress affects the body. Chronic stress can actually influence the way your immune cells function, leading to inflammation. Constant irritations can manifest themselves in various illnesses, including cancer.

Alternatively, per a review published in the *Psychological Bulletin*, positive emotions have been linked to a lower risk of some of the nation's leading causes of death. Psychological well-being makes people less likely to have heart attacks, strokes, and other cardiovascular issues. Negative feelings, on the other hand, often underlie unhealthy habits, such as smoking, drinking, and eating unhealthy diets. People who are happier are usually more flexible and resilient. They cope better with change and disappointment, making them better able to take care of themselves and suffer fewer of the effects of chronic stress.

The contrapositive applies everywhere, including the business world. While working at AT&T, I studied Total Quality Management. When our team was looking at how to make our company successful, we would ask, "How could we fail?" People could easily fill the board with answers. But when we asked how we could succeed, people were stumped. I have continued to conduct this exercise with companies to this day, and it's always the same: lots of reasons for failure, few or none for success.

For whatever reason, we emphasize the negative. We'll tell a bad story seven times, but only tell the good story once.

That's when we'd employ the contrapositive. Once we had all those reasons for failure on the board, we would look at each and reverse engineer them by writing the opposite. That's how we defined success—the opposite of failure. You can do the same. That's how you ultimately create your own battle plan. And that starts with an active and positive mindset.

THE INFLUENCE OF MINDSET: CONTROLLING YOURSELF AND YOUR ENVIRONMENT

Various roles in my life have given me an understanding of the power of mindset. That insight has since allowed me to shape organizations. Combining my corporate and academic experience with my military service gave me a unique perspective.

When I was at the University of South Florida, I took an abnormal psychology class with a wonderful professor, Dr. Stenmark. As I was learning about mental illnesses and their underpinnings, everything seemed to link back to two main ideas: your ability to control yourself, and your ability to control your environment. There's a continuum to this idea. The more you can do of both is good. The less you can do of both is bad. Everything else is somewhere in between.

Think of it like rowing a boat. If you have both oars working, you make a lot of progress in the boat. If you only have one oar rowing, the boat still goes but it doesn't exactly go where you want it to—but even that is okay. But if you lose both oars—the ability to control yourself and to influence your environment—it becomes a real problem.

In the military, I witnessed highly cohesive teams performing at very high levels. The people on these teams had incredible amounts of control and discipline over themselves and an extreme ability to influence their environment. They could *shape* their environment. They could impose their will on the enemy. This illustrates the opposite end of the continuum.

The impact of your environment also depends a great deal on how you interpret it. That's how you cope. Think about the time you have before you die. That's all the time you have left to live a life that matters, and that will be determined in large part by your mindset. Sound depressing? It doesn't have to be.

I saw a famous inventor speak recently, a man who has created a number of new drugs, who estimated that he had about 10,500 days left to live. That knowledge makes him want to use every day wisely. He does smart things to try to prolong his life, but it is in service of his passion: to create an elixir to save children on the brink of starvation. He's got a defensive and an offensive strategy. He's literally counting the days he has left, which could be depressing, but he's doing it in a very purposeful and positive way. He has a good mindset.

We have more power over our lives than we realize, and much of that power comes from our mindset.

MINDSET, HAPPINESS, AND HEALTH

Mindset is critical to being proactive in your own care, and you must be actively engaged in your own care. You have to be able to navigate the system, and you need to understand that there are consequences for failing to do so. Changing your mindset to be active, asking questions, and building your knowledge over time can be life-changing. You don't need the government to pass a law in order to do that. You don't need to make more money. You just need the right mindset.

Just as I suggest you know your health metrics and nutritional requirements, it is also possible to impact and quantify your mindset. The overall data point that reflects mindset is happiness. In 2012, the United Nations issued the first World Happiness Report, a global survey of well-being and happiness that ranks countries from the happiest to least happy.[96] Surprisingly,

---

96 World Happiness Report. http://worldhappiness.report/

generosity, social support, and perceived freedom to make life decisions made up half of the variables that determine a country's happiness score. Likewise, individual happiness can also be measured. Longevity, for example—another contributor to national happiness—is largely determined by an individual's close relationships and social integration.[97] You can actually count the number of friends you have and the organizations you support in your community.

The opposite is also true. Social isolation and loneliness are associated with increased mortality, sickness, and disability in older adults. Research shows that not only do they negatively impact an individual's mindset, they have a physical risk as well: the equivalent of smoking fifteen cigarettes a day.[98] Don't underestimate the value and importance of connectedness.

Our basic temperament is inherited. Despite this, we have some control over how happy we feel. Positive psychologist Sonja Lyubomirsky and her colleagues estimate that happiness is 50 percent inherited. Another 40 percent is under our own power to control. The final 10

---

97 https://www.ted.com/talks/susan_pinker_the_secret_to_living_longer_may_be_your_social_life/ transcript#t-485188

98 https://www.washingtonpost.com/news/on-leadership/wp/2017/10/04/this-former-surgeon-general-says-theres-a-loneliness-epidemic-and-work-is-partly-to-blame/?utm_term=. c744247c88b0

percent depends on circumstances.[99] Mindset can impact happiness, and to the extent that you can control your environment, you can impact your happiness.

As Henry Ford said, "Whether you think you can or think you cannot—you are right."

While social determinants may have little impact on overall happiness, they have a significant impact on health outcomes. As you can see in the following chart, individual behavior is the largest contributor to your overall health, or in this case, your demise. Again, we see the power of the contrapositive.

IMPACT OF DIFFERENT FACTORS ON RISK OF PREMATURE DEATH

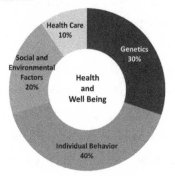

SOURCE: Schroeder, SA. (2007). We Can Do Better — Improving the Health of the American People. *NEJM.* 357:1221-8.

Image courtesy of the Kaiser Family Foundation[100]

---

99   Sonja Lyubomirsky, *The How of Happiness: A New Approach to Getting the Life You Want* (New York: Penguin Press, 2007).

100 Harry J. Heiman and Samantha Artiga, "Beyond Health Care: The Role of Social Determinants in Promoting Health and Health Equity," The Henry J. Kaiser Family Foundation, November 4, 2015, accessed March 14, 2018. https://www.kff.org/disparities-policy/issue-brief/beyond-health-care-the-role-of-social-determinants-in-promoting-health-and-health-equity/

What is interesting to note here is that even though individual behaviors have the biggest impact, they are directly tied to what are called the social determinants of health, as depicted in the next chart. It turns out that your zip code plays a bigger role than your genetic code in your overall well-being.

SOCIAL DETERMINANTS OF HEALTH

Economic Stability	Neighborhood and Physical Environment	Education	Food	Community and Social Context	Health Care System
Employment	Housing	Literacy	Hunger	Social integration	Health coverage
Income	Transportation	Language	Access to healthy options	Support systems	Provider availability
Expenses	Safety	Early childhood education		Community engagement	Provider linguistic and cultural competency
Debt	Parks	Vocational training		Discrimination	
Medical bills	Playgrounds				
Support	Walkability	Higher education			Quality of care

Health Outcomes
Mortality, Morbidity, Life Expectancy, Health Care Expenditures, Health Status, Functional Limitations

Image courtesy of the Kaiser Family Foundation[101]

Healthy People 2020 recognizes that health disparities are rooted in the social, economic, and environmental context in which people live. Children born to parents who have not completed high school are more likely to live in an environment that poses barriers to health. Similarly, lower education levels are directly correlated with

---

101 Harry J. Heiman and Samantha Artiga, "Beyond Health Care: The Role of Social Determinants in Promoting Health and Health Equity," The Henry J. Kaiser Family Foundation, November 4, 2015, accessed February 22, 2018. https://www.kff.org/disparities-policy/issue-brief/beyond-health-care-the-role-of-social-determinants-in-promoting-health-and-health-equity/

lower income, higher likelihood of smoking, and shorter life expectancy.

Creating a preventative and positive mindset in the neighborhoods and communities that need it most can influence a change in individual behaviors, which have the greatest overall impact on health. Lending a hand to these communities will not only improve their outcomes, it will also provide you with a sense of purpose, which will also help you and your health and happiness.

DEVELOPING A PROACTIVE AND POSITIVE MINDSET

Just as we can anticipate and prepare for the time when we get sick or hurt physically, we have to prepare for the time when we may get sick or hurt mentally. We can train and build resilience. We can prepare the mind, perhaps the least understood and most powerful part of the human body. I know people who downsize to a one-story house because they anticipate physical difficulty with stairs as they get older. We also know that eventually we will lose friends and loved ones, yet very few people know much about the mental and emotional difficulty of how to manage the loss or help others to do the same. With one in three Americans likely to face some form of depression, it's probably wise to mentally prepare now. Preparing in the good times can really help you through the bad times.

There is a new field called "positive psychology" that talks about happiness and inner strength. According to *Psychology Today*, "positive psychology is the study of happiness. Psychology has traditionally focused on dysfunction—people with mental illness or other issues—and how to treat it. Positive psychology, by contrast, is a field that examines how ordinary people can become happier and more fulfilled."[102]

In the *Psychology Today* article "What Happy People Do Differently," Robert Biswas-Diener and Todd B. Kashdan suggest:

> The secret of happiness is a concern of growing importance in the modern era, as increased financial security has given many the time to focus on self-growth. No longer hunter-gatherers concerned with where to find the next kill, we worry instead about how to live our best lives. Happiness books have become a cottage industry; personal-development trainings are a bigger business than ever.

Regardless of your emotional set point, your everyday habits and choices—from the way you operate in a friendship to how you reflect on your life decisions—can push the needle on your well-being. Recent scholarship documenting the unique habits of those who are happiest in

---

102 https://www.psychologytoday.com/basics/positive-psychology

life even provides something of an instruction manual for emulating them. It turns out that activities that lead us to feel uncertainty, discomfort, and even a dash of guilt are associated with some of the most memorable and enjoyable experiences of people's lives. Happy people, it seems, engage in a wide range of counterintuitive habits that seem, well, downright *un*happy.

Truly happy people seem to have an intuitive grasp of the fact that sustained happiness is not just about doing things that you like. It also requires growth and adventuring beyond the boundaries of your comfort zone. Happy people, are, simply put, curious. In a 2007 study, Todd Kashdan and Colorado State psychologist Michael Steger found that when participants monitored their own daily activities, as well as how they felt, over the course of twenty-one days, those who frequently felt curious on a given day also experienced the most satisfaction with their life—and engaged in the highest number of happiness-inducing activities, such as expressing gratitude to a colleague or volunteering to help others.[103]

There can be a hedonistic aspect to feeling good—take, for example, the whole idea of "eat, drink, and be merry." You can go out and indulge yourself, and it may be okay

103 Robert Biswas-Diener and Todd B. Kashdan, "What Happy People Do Differently," *Psychology Today*, July 2, 2013. https://www.psychologytoday.com/articles/201307/what-happy-people-do-differently

now and then, and it definitely feels good. The problem is, it's not sustainable. If you did that every day, after a while it wouldn't keep making you feel good. What is sustainable is feeling good by engaging fully and being immersed in something that consumes you. That is a way to happiness: doing what you love. As they say, if you find a job you love, you'll never have to work again. It's also known that doing good, just helping other people and making the world a better place, is fulfilling and leads to happiness.

We all should think about what drives us, what our inner strengths are, and how we can align those with our values and our daily activities. If you're aware of your purpose and you're aligning things that motivate you with your physical health and your mental health, that alignment creates a more fulfilling life. Serve the greater good, be true to your passions, find what you're best at, spend a lot of time doing that, and help others to do so as well. That's how you hack happiness.

AMERICA'S UNIQUE NATURE: A BLESSING AND A CURSE

The United States is unique in many ways. Our ability to beat the odds is unique, as is our ability to be number one in so many things. I once climbed the Leaning Tower of Pisa in Italy. There's a tiny spiral staircase that leads to the very top. Of course, I went up the narrow staircase.

Someone said, "He must be American. The Americans always have to go to the top." He was on a little mezzanine level that was just ten feet below the spiral staircase. And he was right, I think. I am an American, and my goal was to go to the absolute very top. The other people were all hanging out where there was more room, which was more practical, but I wanted to keep going up.

The fact that the United States even made it as a nation, defeating Great Britain in the Revolutionary War, was miraculous. We survived, and we thrived. In World War II, I believe it was the grit, determination, and collective will from those early days that pushed us to victory.

But defying the odds, as much as it's a part of our culture, does not mesh with following a doctor's orders. I remember my dad saying stuff like, "It came by itself; it'll go by itself." This is completely irrational, but it's a way of coping. It's a defense mechanism. But it also reflects the mental toughness of a great generation.

We like to defy the odds. We like the underdog—the person who snatches victory from the jaws of defeat. It's in our sports and almost every facet of our culture. It keeps us strong and in good spirits as we fight against the odds. Unfortunately, this spirit, I think, and the normal defense mechanism of denial, leads a lot of people to noncompliant behavior.

Medical errors are the number three cause of death, but we also cause our own medical errors through noncompliant behavior. When people don't take their medicine properly or abuse it, or simply don't do what their doctor tells them to do, those are major causes of death and suffering as well.

Applying a "defy the odds" mindset to healthcare is a terrible idea if that means we do not follow doctors' orders. It doesn't put us in a position to be successful. However, you improve your odds by changing your behavior and knowing when you're doing something prudent as part of a health strategy or risk management plan.

It's not easy, but it can be done.

CONNECTING ON A HUMAN LEVEL

The CEO and founder of Iora Health, Dr. Rushika Fernandopulle, introduced me to a new way of thinking. If the patients under his care don't follow their doctor's order, they don't just throw their hands up and say, "Well, we told you to do this and you didn't listen!" Instead, they figure there must be more to it. Maybe the instructions weren't clear. Maybe the patient has a hard home life. Maybe some other factor like depression is causing the noncompliant behavior. They continue until they help the patient become well. Compassion is a mindset.

That's very much like the military. During my seven assignments as a unit commander, for example, I was the messenger, counselor, and support system for all kinds of challenging things: death, divorce, terminal illness, and other life events. I cared for those soldiers 24/7. I didn't just care when they showed up to work at seven thirty at the formation. I cared about their home life, finances, and emotional and overall well-being. All of that went into how they would perform when we went to do what we needed to do: fight and win our nation's wars. This was a profound experience. That holistic concept resonated even more deeply with me when I heard Dr. Fernandopulle speak. It made me understand this gap in our system.

Dr. Fernandopulle had moved on from his medical practice to be the CEO in the organization, but when he returned to visit his practice, he saw one of his former patients. She had taken a turn—for the better. She was taking care of herself and looked good. He said it was great to see her doing so well and asked what had caused the change. She talked about her health coach. She said the health coach took an interest in her and cared about her. She said nobody had really cared about her like that before, and she didn't want to let her coach down. She said, "Because someone cared about me, it made me care about myself." Talk about the power of mindset!

As your loved ones enter the healthcare battlefield,

remember the importance of the human connection and the role that you can play to help them maintain a positive mindset. It might be your most important weapon.

ACCEPTING THE INEVITABLE AND RISING TO THE OCCASION

Accepting your own mortality isn't just necessary, it's helpful. A big benefit of facing your own mortality is that it can spur you to get your priorities in order and behave accordingly. When people go into the hospital or have some kind of close call, life starts to take on a new perspective. Better to get that perspective now and avoid that close call altogether. If you have open-heart surgery, for example, it will radically change your lifestyle. Why not make small changes today and avoid an unpleasant tomorrow?

It's especially important to get that positive perspective now, because without it the opposite may happen. You've got to accept what's inevitable, but more importantly, become proactive against what is not inevitable and take back some control. Tackling your mindset, being proactive, and turning things around are hard to do. Yet the fact remains that you are in control of yourself, and you can gain at least some control of your environment. Remember the inventor who counted his days: he embraced the inevitability of his death and turned it into something incredibly positive.

Every day that you wake up, you have the choice to be happy or not. You must see it ultimately as a choice that you make. Life often culminates in something unplanned, and some people aren't mentally prepared for it, which leads to negative emotions. And by the time it happens, they're ill-equipped to be able to influence it. That's why it's important to take steps while you're able and strong enough to prepare.

Making better decisions is a function of being prepared, which is a function of training and planning, and that includes a mental game plan. Remember that your game plan will probably change as you age. It's vital that you choose to actively be in charge of your health at every stage in life. When you wake up, remember, you always have a choice. You can choose to be happy, and you can make and follow a plan. You can choose to be in control.

Nutrition, movement, and mindset are the weapons you have to combat disease on the healthcare battlefield—and they are readily available to you. You must go onto the battlefield prepared. You know what your weapons are. Now it's time to continue your training. You *need to know* how to use them and, in turn, how to help others use them.

If we all work together to eliminate the unnecessary lives lost, suffering, and costs, we will serve the greater good.

We'll be a healthier, happier, and wealthier nation. If I am stronger, the nation is stronger.

The same is true of you.

PART III

GETTING HEALTHCARE TO CARE FOR YOU

CHAPTER 7

WHAT'S WORKING WELL RIGHT NOW

You can't really understand what works well in the health-care system if you do not understand insurance. Just as your lifestyle and well-being are intertwined, so are the choices between your health and health insurance. One way to understand where you are going is to look at where you have been.

In the old days, there was a shift from a feudalistic society to mercantilism. As people learned to sail along the coastlines, they started to exchange goods, like spices and coffee, and it fundamentally changed the way the world worked. Trade routes evolved and created the shipping industry. Coffee houses caught on quickly, and people began to congregate for business, news, and socialization. Over time, coffee houses became "specialized."

Insurance can trace its origins back to the coffee house owned by Edward Lloyd, known for his expertise in the shipping industry, which later became known as Lloyd's of London.[104] Naturally, as the shipping industry grew, so did the number of shipwrecks. It wasn't a question of if; it was a matter of when. And when it happened, a collection was taken for the widow and orphans. An idea was born. Instead of waiting for a shipwreck to happen to collect the funds, it was decided to take a collection from all in advance. The risk was spread or pooled across the group, and in doing so, the insurance industry was created. Insurance is fundamentally good and created for a noble cause.

Health insurance, as we generally think of it in the United States, began with the Great Depression in the 1930s. The Great Depression led hospitals, and then physicians, to implement forms of insurance as means to ensure payment for services. Interestingly, conventional insurance

104 https://www.lloyds.com/about-lloyds/history/corporate-history

and managed care were developed at this same time. The advent of World War II, the growth of the labor movement, and the federal tax code all fostered the growth of employer-sponsored coverage.[105]

Medicare was established in the 1960s as a way to take care of older citizens, regardless of health status or income. Medicare is the cornerstone payer in today's healthcare system.

LOOKING AT MEDICARE OPTIONS

In today's system, you have roughly three choices. You must educate yourself and understand the consequences of the different options, because your decision will directly impact your health and well-being.

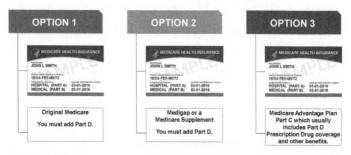

Option 1: Generally speaking, you become eligible for Original Medicare when you turn sixty-five, if you've worked and paid your taxes, or earlier if you have certain disabilities. One of the biggest misconceptions people

105 https://www.ache.org/pubs/Morrisey2253_Chapter_1.pdf

have is that when they get their Medicare, it pays for everything, but that's just not the case. You are subject to cost sharing, co-payments, and multiple benefit-period deductibles. There is no yearly limit for what you pay out-of-pocket. There is no safety net here; your liability is unlimited. The number one cause of bankruptcies are medical bills.

Option 2: Many people find Original Medicare insufficient and choose a Medicare Supplement plan, also known as a Medigap policy, to fill in the gaps of Medicare coverage. These supplemental policies were designed for the episodic-care model, and they are good if you can afford them. They are easy to use, and you probably won't need to go into your pocket much, so people tend to overuse them. The real concern is that they do not offer a coordinated care model, and this is where a lot of the medical errors and costs originate. If you have several doctors who do not talk to each other, they may duplicate services or, even worse, not provide the preventative ones in the first place.

Option 3: The third option is Medicare Advantage, also known as Medicare Part C, and is the epitome of a coordinated care model. It is very affordable, although there are some strings attached. You must pick a primary-care doctor to serve as your quarterback and use the designated "network" of hospitals and specialists. Most Medicare

Advantage plans offer extra coverage, like vision, hearing, dental, and other health and wellness programs. Most also include Medicare prescription drug coverage (Part D).

Medicare Advantage enrollees exceed 20 million members, and membership is expected to grow over the next decade, rising to 41 percent of all Medicare beneficiaries by 2027.[106] This is attributed to the merits of a coordinated care system.

THE BEST OF BOTH WORLDS

One of the best things working right now is the stability, dependability, backing, and oversight of the federal government, combined with the choice, innovation, and high level of efficiency and customer satisfaction that only well-run private companies can offer. It's the best of both worlds. A private insurance company makes more money if it keeps you healthy. The private company puts money into the equation—in some cases, thousands of dollars more in benefits per year than you would get on original Medicare—because they know they'll get that on the back end.

Private companies actually want you to go to the doctor. As you sign up for the plan, they want you to go get a wellness

---

106 https://www.kff.org/medicare/issue-brief/
medicare-advantage-2017-spotlight-enrollment-market-update/

visit. They want you to go to the gym, and they want you to take nutritional supplements if you need them. Two of the biggest things harming the population are smoking and obesity. These companies have programs designed to help you quit smoking and lose weight.

It's not that health plans are philanthropic in nature— although some are. What they do is more efficient because the government is going to pay them the same amount of money whether you get sick or not, because through the Medicare Advantage program, the government pays a fixed amount of money per member, per month. An ounce of prevention beats a pound of cure.

If you're an active person and utilize the benefits of your plan, like a gym membership and nutritional supplements, it may cost the carrier $800 per month. People who aren't active in their own health, who don't exercise or eat right, and aren't educated about using the plan may cost the carrier $6,000 per month. That's eight times more per month spent on a person who isn't active and engaged.

With Medicare Advantage plans, the interests of business, government, and society are aligned. The corporation makes more money because you stay healthier, so they can cover more people. The government has done its job and cared for you. And you live a better life because you're healthier. Everybody wins.

Efficient healthcare requires your participation. This is where we can all help. What if we all inspired our family, friends, and neighbors to get active in their care and the community? This is how we eliminate cost—and we are talking big numbers here.

COORDINATING CARE

The coordinated care model directly cures what ails us. In Chapter 1, I listed some examples of waste in the system, such as unnecessary services, missed prevention, and inefficiently delivered services. Coordinated care models address these inefficiencies, representing hundreds of billions of dollars in savings through improved outcomes. Per an article in the Library of Medicine database, coordinated care models may offer "greater efficiency while attaining equal or superior quality through their flexibility in enrollee benefits, network contracting, and coordination of care."[107] Let's take a closer look at how this could be, with an example of uncoordinated care.

Clare is a sixty-seven-year-old woman in pretty good health, with high blood pressure and a mild case of COPD, who develops a fever and a cough. She can't get in to see her doctor, so she stops by her local pharmacy and buys over-the-counter medication. Unfortunately, her symptoms worsen and, not knowing what else to do,

---

107 https://www.ncbi.nlm.nih.gov/pmc/articles/PMC3587962/

she calls 911 and is transported to the emergency room. While in the emergency room, treating physicians do not have access to Clare's medical history and records. She is prescribed medication, given lab orders for blood work, directed to see her primary-care physician, and discharged. At her primary-care physician appointment, without the ER records, her doctor does not know she was in the emergency room. Clare forgot to get her blood work done and is unable to remember the details of her ER visit. Clare's new medication causes a negative drug interaction with her current prescription, which causes her to get dizzy. She falls, breaks her hip, and is readmitted to the hospital in the intensive care unit.[108] But it doesn't have to be this way.

Now imagine Clare is a member of a Medicare Advantage plan that works with one of the innovative coordinated care organizations that partners with hospitals and physicians. To see an integrated approach to health and wellness, let's rewind the story. When Clare joins the healthcare plan, the first thing she receives is an in-home health assessment that gives her doctors a comprehensive look at her healthcare needs and schedules an appointment with her primary-care physician. During this visit, she is enrolled in a managed-care program for chronic obstructive pulmonary disease (COPD). When a fever and cough come on, she has immediate access to care

108 Scenario adapted from Alignment Healthcare video: https://vimeo.com/128168117

because they know the sensitivity of her condition. Even though her primary-care physician is unavailable, she can still see a doctor who has access to her medical records. Based on tests done in the physician's office, it is immediately determined that Clare has the flu. Her doctor recommends home monitoring, which sends biometric information to the care center daily, so they can monitor Clare's condition. Should Clare's condition worsen, an alert is sent to her primary-care physician, so they will know immediately and can determine the next steps. In this coordinated scenario, there is no adverse drug interaction, no slip and fall, nor readmission to the hospital.

This is how we save lives, avoid misery, and eliminate cost, and it is happening today across the nation. Innovative, coordinated care-delivery models focus on prevention and improved health outcomes. People are literally healthier, happier, and wealthier—and so is our nation.

COORDINATED CARE EVOLUTION: SPECIAL NEEDS PROGRAMS

Having plans that are affordable and coordinated and that provide preventative services and education is a really good thing, and it's something we should be proud of. As I've mentioned before, a small percentage of the population consumes a large percentage of healthcare resources, and the lower income and lower educated segments are hit hardest. Diseases disproportionately attack this segment of the population—any number of studies have shown that lifestyle, income level, and education level correlate with vulnerability to diseases. Medicare Advantage plans are serving the people who need healthcare most, and because these plans have low premiums, sometimes no premium at all, they can attract those people who need healthcare the most.

These disparities don't get enough attention.

Let's take a look, again, at type 2 diabetes. This disease is largely preventable and disproportionately attacks a vulnerable segment of the population. It is miserable for the person who has it and costs society approximately $300 billion a year.[109] The disease attacks several different parts of the body, including the feet, eyes, and kidneys. Each of those parts of the body has a different specialist (podiatrist, ophthalmologist, and nephrologist, to name a few) because that is how doctors are organized.

The bright spot here is that some comprehensive care models are organized around the disease rather than the individual medical professionals. There are different drugs involved, nutritional needs, exercise needs, medical supplies, and management of the overall program to tie

---

109 http://www.diabetes.org/diabetes-basics/statistics/infographics/adv-staggering-cost-of-diabetes.html

it all together. It is a full-time job to see all those people and manage this disease.

Type 2 diabetes management proves to be a great example of the success of a coordinated care model and a specific example where government, health plans, and providers work together to create something called special needs plans (SNPs). These plans are tailored to fit the needs of people with diabetes through health management, prescriptions, and nutritional guidance. A primary-care physician is the quarterback of the care team, coordinating treatment with multiple specialists to create a play that works best for the member.

The government has authorized fifteen special needs plans to serve the chronic-care needs ailing the population. These plans epitomize what is right in our healthcare system today. SNPs are approved by Medicare and run by private companies. When you join a Medicare SNP, you get all your hospital, doctor, and prescription drug coverage through that plan. Perhaps most convenient of all, these benefits are coordinated so you don't have an endless administrative burden.

Another special needs plan is based on income, not a particular disease. This plan is tailored for individuals who are dually eligible for both Medicare and Medicaid. It eliminates a significant administrative burden for the individual by coordinating the availability of doctors' services, billing, and payment of the two programs. It also helps address challenges associated with lower income by providing additional services like no-cost transportation, dental and vision benefits, and monthly allowances to purchase things like Band-Aids and vitamins.

The problem is that most people aren't aware of these packages or programs. It's a matter of education. There are benefits available that people don't know about. People are surprised when I tell them about special needs plans. There was a special needs plan for diabetics in Orlando, Florida, that was a superior product. It didn't cost the member any money out of pocket, and it offered a great network of specialists. It had everything put together, but it didn't sell. It turned out that people just weren't educated about it, and insurance agents didn't know how it worked. Lack of knowledge killed what was a great product in that county.

Still, special needs plans have been growing and today make up almost 15 percent of the Medicare Advantage plans out there. I hope that trend continues.

ALIGNING THE INCENTIVES

Incentives should be aligned with desired behaviors. The interests of business, government, and society need to be aligned. Paying for performance is good for all the stakeholders because prevention beats cure. When you align the incentives, you play to the strengths, and everyone has a role. Individuals, physicians, and insurance plans all have different responsibilities and motivations.

Although the intrinsic value of being healthy and fit should be its own motivation, somehow people need more. Healthy rewards programs help encourage, develop, and incentivize healthy habits. Physical challenges like step contests tap into positive social support and healthy competition. Participants receive discounts on healthy food purchases to promote better nutrition choices. Members earn points for workouts, health and wellness screenings, dental and vision exams, and prevention activities, and the points result in real dollars in their pocket. Overall, these programs foster a healthy mindset and reinforce the basics of wellness.

Much like the individual, some providers also have the opportunity to earn more money when they keep you healthier. Preventing illness or managing it when it comes is personally gratifying to the caregiver and is economically beneficial. There are different compensation models, and the model matters. Some doctors spend more time upfront with a patient and see fewer patients, while other doctors need to see as many patients as possible. Chronic-care models are patient-focused, and doctors are incentivized to have fewer patients and keep them healthier. How does your doctor get paid?

Health plans get paid differently too. Insurance providers are motivated to bring an economic rationality to the business of healthcare. They simply make more money by keeping us healthy. Plans are rated annually based upon members staying healthy through screenings, tests, and vaccines; members managing chronic conditions; plan responsiveness and care; member complaints; and customer service. Because plans are measured this way, insurance providers are motivated to work with good doctors and share best practices.

Government deserves a lot of credit for aligning pay with performance and defining meaningful metrics based on results for physicians, hospitals, and carriers. They reward quality, coordination, and cost effectiveness, perhaps best highlighted by the publicly reported Star Rating System. They also work well with important nonprofit organizations, such as the National Committee for Quality Assurance (NCQA), who compile the Health Effectiveness Data and Information Set (HEDIS) scores driving accountability. This is a big step to helping the healthcare industry evolve by aligning incentives.

TOUGH CHOICES

As I mentioned, when my mom turned sixty-five some time ago, I was vice president at a company. I had an MBA, was a major in the Army Reserves, and knew something about the healthcare industry with my background. When she asked me for help, I was embarrassed to admit I was confused. She had to make some important, complicated choices, and she had a limited window of time in which to make them. When people are scared or confused, the tendency is to freeze up and do nothing. I turned to Nick, a friend of mine, for help, and we got her enrolled in a suitable plan. But not everybody has a friend like Nick. What happens to them?

The fact that the decision is time-sensitive and the issues are complex can make enrolling in Medicare and making the associated choices overwhelming. The stakes are high, adding to the stress. Recently, one of the agents met with a sixty-eight-year-old woman who had mobility issues, could not drive, and was usually confined to a chair. Even though she was enrolled in a plan, this woman had not been to see a doctor in four or five years. Her doctor was forty miles away from where she lived, and there was a several-month wait for an appointment. We found her a doctor much nearer that also offered transportation service, and a plan with a zero premium and very little in the way of out-of-pocket costs. We scheduled an appointment for her and within a week she was there. What if she hadn't found us? What if we had not found her?

You must have a primary-care physician who is your quarterback and your coach. That's fundamental—having somebody on your team, helping you coordinate and navigate the system. Coordinated care models are more efficient and yield better results. Forward-thinking models are also paying more attention to the human element—to the value of connecting and engaging with patients as people, particularly the most vulnerable. That impacts overall outcomes, but it can get overlooked in the wrong model of care.

The healthcare consumer must be active. You need to know why you're picking a particular plan, doctor, or hospital. We can do this now thanks to the Star Rating System. But again, just because we provide you the tools, doesn't mean that the house is going to build itself. A professional health agent is well positioned to help you understand the tools available, identify the right plan, and choose an appropriate care provider. You must make an effort to educate yourself to make such choices and to discipline yourself to make reasonable efforts to build a better you through nutrition, movement, and mindset.

STAR RATING SYSTEM[110]

The government is working to compensate for quality and for outcomes and to allow people to know whether a particular health plan is of high quality, and so they've come up with a Star Rating System. The ratings take into account quality, including customer satisfaction and many other important things. Five stars is the best rating you can get. Two stars ultimately means that after enough time goes by without improvement, that plan will no longer be in business. This is good because it means the ability to shop around will improve, as will the ability to know what quality you're getting as a consumer. It's outcomes that matter, and the Star Rating System recognizes that.

---

110 https://www.cms.gov/Newsroom/MediaReleaseDatabase/Fact-sheets/2016-Fact-sheets-items/2016-10-12.html

CHAPTER 8

TECHNOLOGY

NEED-TO-KNOW NUGGETS

- Moore's Law tells us that computer processing power doubles every eighteen months, while shrinking in cost.
- Eight technologies are converging to change the world.
- Policy and adoption of innovative technologies can take more than a decade to move into the mainstream.
- "The future has arrived—it's just not evenly distributed yet." (William Gibson)

Let's start by saying this: technology is changing everything. The way we drive, the way we eat, the way we do pretty much everything. But the technologies we read about every day in the paper are also changing the way we are looking—and will look—at healthcare. The eight technologies I'm discussing here are going to have a profound impact on how the world will change.

Computer chips are everywhere and can be found in more devices every day. Moore's Law traces back to an observation made by Gordon Moore in 1955. He observed that the number of transistors per square inch on an integrated circuit board was continually increasing, tending to double every twelve to eighteen months. As computing power gets more powerful, it also gets cheaper. The first computers once took up entire floors, and now your smartphone has more computing power in it than the Apollo 7 rocket. Moore's Law continues to hold true to this day, though some predict we may reach a limit soon beyond which there will be no physical room left at such small scales to keep doubling. But I think nanotechnology (more on this in a moment) will allow this to continue.

Microchips are in everything—cars, refrigerators, and of course your phone. Few devices nowadays don't have some sort of a chip inside them. Computing power is a matter of national security. With access and enough computer power, you can hack anything from passwords to power plants. There are even laws today against exporting powerful chips to other countries.

Technology moves much faster than the policies and laws surrounding it do. We have technologies emerging today that are barely understood. It will be a long time before we begin putting the right laws and rules around them. It can take a decade for the adoption of new technologies to get to the point where they're accepted into the mainstream and your local physician is able to offer them to you. Right now, you can genetically engineer babies, but the people who make the laws don't even understand what's happening well enough to make rules about it. There are cancer therapies today that take your own T-cells and reprogram them so they know to find the cancer and use your own immune system to kill the cancer. But that's new, and in practical terms, it will be a long time before your local doctor is likely to promote it, even though the FDA has already approved it.

The relentless increase in computing power is behind a lot of technological advances today. But beyond that, I would like to talk about eight emerging technologies that are impacting the world. Many of these extend beyond the healthcare realm, although they have healthcare applications. These technologies are evolving at a pace that's never been seen before. Any one of them would be powerful on its own, but together they are exponentially disruptive to the system in a good way.

Let me bring up a military analogy. In the 1700s, you'd pack powder into your musket and insert the cap and musket ball and fire.[111] If you were good, you could maybe get a few shots off in a minute. Then the rifle was invented in the mid-1800s, which involved loading a cartridge. This

---

111 https://www.military.com/army-birthday/history-of-us-army-weapons.html

new rifle technology shot roughly twice as far while being significantly more accurate. You could shoot rounds ten times faster. In warfare, technological innovations have been a significant factor in who wins battles. The same has been true and will continue to be true when it comes to healthcare.

My own experience with the military involved the use of *biometrics*, which you may know something about from police crime dramas. Detectives search a crime scene for clues like fingerprints, saliva, hair, and anything that may have traces of DNA on it. Matching up those human characteristics with someone's identity involves biometrics. A bomb blast is really a crime scene in a lot of ways, and terrorists are often more like criminals than soldiers. When I was in Afghanistan catching bad guys, the DNA analyzer we were using was huge and cost about a million dollars. Years later when I was working with the Criminal Investigation Division, our desktop unit and field lab were down to a couple of hundred thousand dollars each and were each the size of a desktop computer. Right now, they're down to about $5,000 and are the size of your phone. Technology is constantly getting better, faster, smaller, and cheaper. We've seen this time and time again.

When I was at AT&T, we got into the web-content hosting business because the central switching office from the phone companies had gotten so small that our buildings had entire empty floors. We had a building in downtown Manhattan that was pretty much empty because what used to take multiple floors of a building to process the telephone calls had shrunk down to a tiny box. AT&T used to run the communications network for the country (which, at the time, was just the phone system). Its facilities were hardened because of the Russian nuclear threat. All through the 1950s and 1960s, the company built fortified facilities to withstand a blast so we could still use our phones to communicate if there was ever an attack. Now those buildings were essentially empty and were sitting on top of the big pipe that voice, video, and data runs on today. It was easy for AT&T to put some hosting servers on the now-empty floors and connect them directly to the internet using a single pipe.

Such examples of technological changes give us hints about what is coming in healthcare. I think that in our lifetime we're going to see incredible things—equivalent to putting a man on the moon—that will be enabled by technology and by people working together.

It will happen everywhere, including healthcare.

THE INTERNET OF THINGS

A book called *When Things Start to Think* by Neil Gershenfeld came out in 1999. It was about how everyday machines would start to communicate with each other. For example, you could take something out of your refrigerator and it would automatically reorder it for you if you didn't put it back in. As predicted, the Internet of Things (IoT) has indeed begun to happen. Products containing little sensors with microchips that communicate via the Internet are widespread already. The idea of sensors comes, of course, from the human body. Your eyes, your nose, your skin, and your nerves are sensors. The history of using tools to improve our sense goes way back—to telescopes and eyeglasses, for example. Some electronic sensors go beyond those of the human body. Imaging technology can see better than the human eye. One emerging powerful aspect of the IoT comes from its ability to collect large amounts of data. It could change the way medical care is delivered.

Even though the healthcare industry has been slower to adopt Internet of Things technologies than other industries, the Internet of Medical Things (IoMT) is poised to transform how we keep people safe and healthy, especially as the demand for solutions to lower healthcare costs increases in the coming years. The IoMT can help monitor, inform, and notify healthcare providers with real-time data to identify issues before they become critical or to allow for earlier intervention. "Today, there are 3.7 million medical devices in use that are connected to and monitor various parts of the body to inform healthcare decisions."[112]

Imagine being able to detect cancer within minutes. The IoT and its sensors and networks can help identify leading indicators, as opposed to lagging indicators. The horse that won a race is a *lagging* indicator. *Leading* indicators are clues that can be picked up early and that could help predict the winner before the race begins. With cancer, it turns out that before a tumor turns cancerous, before there can even be said to be cancer present in the first place, cells form a little colony.[113] That colony grows and becomes cancerous over time, sometimes for years. If you had the right sensor and could detect and measure such colonies properly, you would likely be able to identify and head off cancer.

The sensors collect the information, but it's networks that aggregate and allow you to process that data and make it meaningful and useful.

---

112 Bernard Marr, "Why the Internet of Medical Things (IoMT) Will Start to Transform Healthcare in 2018," Forbes, January 25, 2018. https://www.forbes.com/sites/bernardmarr/2018/01/25/why-the-internet-of-medical-things-iomt-will-start-to-transform-healthcare-in-2018/#66f0a0b54a3c

113 Michio Kaku, "The World in 2030: How Science Will Affect Computers, Medicine, Jobs, Our Lifestyles and the Wealth of our Nations," video, December 15, 2009. https://www.youtube.com/watch?v=219YybX66MY

CLOUD COMPUTING

When I was at IBM, we were talking about the "cloud" back in the 1990s. The cloud consists of a network of connected sensors and processors that work together online. It doesn't matter where any particular machine is located, hence "cloud." Cloud computation aggregates the data from all those sensors. Just as it doesn't matter where any particular machine in the cloud is located geographically, the sensors and processors can be all over the place too. The data and the sensor can *both* be almost anywhere. Being able to know what's happening somewhere else without actually being there solves the time/distance problem. If you need more computing capability, you can add that from another place, too. That's what cloud computing makes possible.

This is already happening with facial recognition. If authorities are looking for a particular bad guy—a nefarious character, as we used to call them—they can run facial recognition and a match may pop up almost anywhere. A camera somewhere found a pattern, and, sure enough, that person was there. We may be able to do something similar with sensors, databases of the human genome, and electronic medical records.

Such technologies will help us be able to anticipate things before they happen. They'll also help us make faster and more accurate decisions. Doctors will be able to make diagnoses faster. Think about when NASA or SpaceX launches a vehicle into space. You see the nerve center with dozens of people all watching the screen, monitoring the performance. Caregivers may be able to do something similar, using the cloud to monitor sensors that are tracking your health. In the evolving chronic-care model, as I've discussed throughout, we have to anticipate things. Predicting the future is hard, but computation and algorithms help tremendously. Connecting information, no matter where it resides, is enabled by cloud computing.

3-D PRINTING

Consider how something like the International Space Station was built. They had to launch payloads containing everything they needed, which is expensive and inefficient. If something breaks up there, it's a bit hard to go down to the store and pick up a replacement, so you've got to bring a spare or two of most everything. Three-dimensional printers will solve that problem. Three-dimensional printers are like little on-demand factories. They make things on the spot. Three-dimensional printing is going to fundamentally disrupt the supply chain of products worldwide. The whole idea of making something in a factory, shipping it halfway around the world on a boat, driving it along highways on a truck, and delivering it to a store where consumers have to drive to buy it, is all going to change.

In the not-too-distant future, you'll have a 3-D printer in your home, just like you probably have a printer for your computer right now, that can manufacture almost anything. When you break the caster on your chair, for example, you can just "print" a new one. It may seem far-fetched, but many didn't think we would have regular printers in our homes either.

Three-dimensional printers will be able to print many different things—even our food. And that's important. Food and nutrition are other important areas. The world population is well over 7 billion, on its way to 8 billion people. Being able to produce enough food to feed them all, especially proteins from animals, is a problem we're going to have to face. The oceans are already running out of fish.[114] We'll need other sources. Much of the world gets its protein from sources like beans. Three-dimensional printers could begin printing meat-like food items using something like bean protein.

Perhaps even more interesting, they can print bodily organs. Cellink[115], for example, is just one company that, using something called bioink,[116] is able to print organs like noses and ears. Mixed with human cells, the "ink"

114 https://www.smithsonianmag.com/videos/category/science/
     the-ocean-is-running-out-of-fish-heres-the/

115 https://cellink.com/bioprinter/

116 https://cellink.com/bioink/

provides an environment for the cells to grow, and it's only the beginning. Organs wear out, but we're already printing them. Since 2012, there have been people walking around with organs that were grown on latticework made by a 3-D printer.

ROBOTS AND DRONES

In California, I recently saw a 3-D printer that could print a robot.[117] The robot could then operate the 3-D printer. That's available today. Imagine where that kind of thing will go in the future. People are familiar with industrial robots, which build things like your car. But not all robots are big. Some are small—very small. They're called *nanobots*, and one day they will be able to put nanobots inside of you that will help you fight off pathogens. It's a tremendously exciting idea from a medical point of view. Robots can also be used on the outside of the body—to augment the skeleton, for example. Robots can help people walk again. As the robotics improve, imagine a spine that can't be repaired. An exoskeleton robot can augment the spine's function. Check out the robotic exoskeleton that helps people walk: https://www.cnn.com/2013/05/22/tech/innovation/exoskeleton-robot-suit/index.html.[118]

Artificial limbs already have very lifelike dexterity. Some-

117 https://m.all3dp.com/1/3d-printed-robot-print-robots/

118 https://www.cnn.com/2013/05/22/tech/innovation/exoskeleton-robot-suit/index.html

thing like replacing Luke Skywalker's hand in the Star Wars movies with an artificial hand that's nearly as good is likely to become reality.

We've all heard that drones could soon be dropping off packages at customers' doors, but imagine if they could also save your life. Recently, off the coast of Australia, a drone was used to drop a floatation device to swimmers who were in trouble, saving their lives. Better yet, Swedish researchers are using drones to carry automated external defibrillators (AED) to people who are in cardiac arrest. The more time a person spends in cardiac arrest before being shocked with an AED, the lower the chance of survival. Shocking someone within three minutes gives them the best shot. More than 350,000 cardiac arrests happen across the US in places other than hospitals each year, according to the American Heart Association—and a person's chance of surviving is about one in ten. Drone-delivered AEDs beat ambulance trip times to the scenes of cardiac arrests, according to the *Journal of the American Medical Association*.[119]

ARTIFICIAL INTELLIGENCE

Artificial Intelligence (AI) is probably the most interesting emerging technology. Ray Kurzweil and many other futurists predict that machines will one day become smarter

---

119 https://jamanetwork.com/journals/jama/fullarticle/2631520

than humans, causing a lot of controversy and bringing with it many moral implications. We all know that IBM's Deep Blue beat the chess player Garry Kasparov back in 1996. Now it turns out that as machines learn to think, they can also teach themselves things. Facebook has discovered that AIs create their own languages when talking to each other, leaving behind human-created languages, and the engineers really have no idea what the machines are saying.[120] Google and others already have autonomous vehicles driving around parts of California. In a matter of a few years, I believe self-driving cars will be available in several major cities, starting in Las Vegas.

Who is the driver in those cases? The National Transportation Safety Board (NTSB) is considering the artificial intelligence itself to be the driver. They passed regulations recently, and now these cars are in fact able to drive. How might that impact healthcare? Well, over 37,000 people a year die in car accidents,[121] often because of driver error. Technology will reduce these errors. Keep in mind that each time a machine crashes and kills someone, it will be publicized dramatically, but the truth is that a lot of people probably shouldn't be driving today because their sensors and processing abilities—meaning their eyes and response time—have degraded. This will provide them a better alternative.

---

120 https://futurism.com/a-facebook-ai-unexpectedly-created-its-own-unique-language/

121 https://www.ntsb.gov/investigations/data/Pages/Data_Stats.aspx

Artificial intelligence is in its infancy now, but it will pay real dividends for us down the road. Expert systems will help caregivers make better, more accurate, faster decisions. Radiologists, for example, use their sensors (eyes) to examine medical imaging to diagnose and treat disease. But even an experienced radiologist who has expertly examined tens of thousands of images can only see so well and no better. An AI on the cloud would have access to millions upon millions of images, as well as to perhaps all radiology studies ever done. It could see with better optics and draw conclusions based on a superior data set. Already studies suggest that such machines may be 40 percent better at catching things than humans are.[122] A common error in radiology occurs when a radiologist overlooks something that's there. They either don't see it, or they see it but don't realize what it is. Computers just see better. I'm not saying machines will ever replace doctors, but automating tasks and drudgery can't help but free up medical professionals to focus and spend more time with patients. AI is an enabling technology that will bring great benefits to the healthcare field.

MATERIALS SCIENCE

Materials science is advancing rapidly. These scientists are making new materials, never seen before. I was rowing in a crew boat recently that was old and used, but still

---

122 http://republic-of-innovation.ch/ibms-watson-could-diagnose-cancer-better-than-doctors/

cost $22,000. A bigger one that could board eight people might cost $50,000. Why so much? Because the carbon fiber compound they're made of is light and strong. This compound has been designed and refined over time so that world-class Olympic rowers can go out and compete. Scientists and engineers are diving deep into the stuff of matter, manipulating molecules and components of molecules to create things that didn't exist before.

In short, that means we can now build things we couldn't build before. For example, some people are walking around on titanium hips today. Entire joints can be replaced with amazing materials. And as the new materials develop, they're only going to get better. For example, nanotechnology, which is largely based on materials science, has created a gel that spurs the growth of nerve cells and could eventually be used to regrow lost or damaged brain cells.[123]

We believe we'll be able to make many nanobio building blocks that nature provided for us—collagen, nanocellulose, resilin, and many more. These will enable us to make better machines, even the heart. This heart is not going to be the same as we can get from a donor. It actually will perform better and will last longer.[124]

---

123 http://nano4me.org/handbook/QbC.pdf

124 Oded Shoseyov, "How We're Harnessing Natures Hidden Superpowers," video, September 28, 2016. https://www.ted.com/talks/oded_shoseyov_how_we_re_harnessing_nature_s_hidden_superpowers/transcript#t-852072

VIRTUAL AND AUGMENTED REALITY

We've probably all seen virtual reality (VR) gaming goggles by now. *Virtual reality* fully immerses you in a virtual world. *Augmented reality* (AR) adds a visual layer on top of what you see in the real world. I put on a pair of augmented reality goggles when I was out in California and sat on a stool. My friend came up and grabbed me by the shoulder to hold me, telling me he had tried it and nearly fell off the stool. In this version of reality, I was in the same room, but I was very small, and was presented with a visual of being on a roller-coaster. I first had the sensation of moving forward on a track. Then I dropped down, and the device truly tricked my senses, giving me the sensation that I really was swooping down on a roller coaster right there in the room! Then I went around what looked like a little race-car track, and then it shot me underneath the couch, and I literally ducked because I was so small in the augmented reality. It was unbelievably exhilarating. The sensors of your body can definitely be manipulated.

We must also be careful to acknowledge the emotional and psychological consequences as we use technology to impact our reality. Although the situation is not real because the technology tricks us, the biological and emotional response is very real. Nicole Kidman, who stars in the series *Big Little Lies*, talks about the emotional distress she was under after filming violent scenes and how she had to talk herself out of that state of mind.[125] In a way, these actors tap into their own version of augmented reality to produce these emotions on demand.

Virtual and augmented reality is an exciting field, and its technologies can be used in many different ways. The entertainment possibilities should be obvious, but it's great for military and medical training, and education in general. Schoolchildren can "experience" new countries without going there. For example, they can put on goggles and have the sensation of being on the Serengeti plain in Africa—one of my favorite places.

In the medical field, these VR and AR technologies are already used in teaching and demonstrations. You put the glasses on and you're looking at the cells as if you're inside the body. The 1966 movie *Fantastic Voyage*—in which people are miniaturized and travel through a living human being in a tiny ship—was an early hint of what we're seeing today in real life. In the movie, the white blood cells attack them, and they move through the heart. Now the pharmaceutical industry is using this kind of tech in their research, looking at molecules and inhibitors. Today you can swallow a camera sensor that images your digestive tract as it passes through it, providing an incredibly close and detailed look at the entire digestive

125 http://www.etonline.com/tv/222424_nicole_kidman_talks_going_home_to_keith_urban_loving_arms_after_tough_big_little_lies_scenes

system. Such cameras will only get smaller and better and will be applied in ways we probably can't imagine today.

SYNTHETIC BIOLOGY

Synthetic biology is about genetic reprogramming. There was a case where a child had leukemia. All the treatments had failed, and the child's prognosis was, unfortunately, death. But doctors were able to take out T cells and send them to a lab, where a computer helped them alter the DNA. They put a message in the cells to allow them to recognize cancer and injected those T cells back into the child. There remained some safety concerns with an experimental treatment like that because it hadn't yet been fully studied, but in this case, death was otherwise certain, so it was worth the risk. It worked; the child lived. You might want to check out some of the work bluebird bio is doing to cure some of the 7,000 childhood diseases.[126]

Some people are born genetically "rich" and some are born genetically "poor." Adding computing power to the mapping of the human genome enables reprogramming of cells, but that leads to ethical issues too. Should we have designer babies, for example? If we're able to edit genes, will we see a world of rich people who can take advantage of that technology and poor people who can't?

---

126 https://www.bluebirdbio.com/

The laws and regulations around this technology will be very interesting to watch unfold.

THE LAG IN ADOPTING NEW TECHNOLOGIES

For years it's been known that a person who has congestive heart failure typically gained ten pounds in weight as a precursor to their heart attack.[127] If you're recording your weight and suddenly gain ten pounds, that could well be an indicator. Earlier in this chapter, I talked about how sensors can help find leading versus lagging indicators. In healthcare, sensors in the home are likely to help find important leading indicators. For example, there are sensors now that you can put in your mirror that can pick up blood glucose on your breath. That could save a lot of painful finger sticks.

The solutions surrounding telemedicine—treating or diagnosing patients remotely—that I've seen in place are still clunky. The devices aren't updated, liability issues are involved, and there are laws about practicing medicine across state lines. Policy issues around telemedicine need to be brought up to speed. I have an alarm system at my office and home. If something opens or closes that isn't supposed to, I know about it. Sometimes it's a routine thing. I know someone went into the office on Sunday, and I knew they were going to do that because we had

---

127 http://circ.ahajournals.org/content/116/14/1549

something we had to do on Monday. It just told me that the person came and went, so I knew it wasn't an alarm—it was just information.

People with chronic conditions can use sensor technologies to predict things. A few innovative care models are starting to do this. Doctors put the sensors in place wherever they're needed to monitor the patient's body, and use the information gathered as part of a diabetes-management program. These people aren't brought into the hospital and put into the intensive care unit. They're remotely monitored. I always joke that, ultimately, the ambulance will come to your house before you need it and say it was worried about you because sensors are indicating trouble. That, to me, is how proactive monitoring should play out.

But adopting new technologies takes time. Sometimes it takes a long time. Many people remain in the dark about how medicine is evolving. If you look at what most people know about their own health, and then you look at the systems and tools that are already in place or coming soon, we really have not evolved very much. What is possible today isn't being implemented, and people are dying unnecessarily. A lot of misery and cost could be avoided if we could just embrace these technologies faster.

People must become more educated and choose health

plans with proven results. We must demand best-in-class care and tolerate nothing less. We must stay informed of the latest advances and actively seek them out. This will significantly improve our odds and potentially save hundreds of billions of dollars.

As the science fiction writer William Gibson has quipped, "The future is here, it's just not equally distributed."

CHAPTER 9

HEALTHCARE MODEL FOR THE FUTURE

NEED-TO-KNOW NUGGETS

- Personalized healthcare is the future.
- Living and dying on your own terms.

When I was working at United States Special Operations Command (USSOCOM), conducting vulnerability assessments, we had some incredible tools. I was able to assess the vulnerability of a particular building and had software to model various scenarios. For example, I could enter the exact materials the building was made of and accurately predict what a truck loaded with 200 pounds of C-4 parked outside of the front door would do to the structure and people inside. Based on this exact analysis, I could go back and mitigate the risk by doing things like placing barriers (bollards) out front to create a clear zone between the vehicles and the building. I could also laminate the windows, so the glass would not shatter in a blast to harm the people inside. As you can imagine, it would go on like that until we felt we had adequately protected the facility.

In the future, it will be the same in healthcare. We will be able to take your human genome, the microbiome, your environment, and any other pertinent information and create a computer simulation that is the digital version of you. With this model, you will be able to run scenarios to determine what is ideal for you. Your doctor will be able to model treatments, medicines, and other care plans. You will be able to model lifestyle choices, and a particular diet or exercise program. You will be able to use artificial intelligence to accurately anticipate and optimize the results. When you can "see" the immediate link between cause and effect of your new behavior, it will increase your motivation.

We are seeing this in other industries today. My wife bought a pair of tennis shoes recently—but it was a very different experience from what many of us are used to: going to the store, trying on the best pair we see, and being satisfied with what we found. No, my wife was able to customize her Adidas exactly how she wanted them— colors, material, even custom writing on the side. She also has an app on her phone that lets her see what she'd look like with different hairstyles before she takes the risk and spends the money on a new do. Why do I say this? Because industries everywhere now are *personalized*. It makes sense.

We even see this in farming now. Benjamin Netanyahu, the prime minister of Israel, talked in an interview recently about how sensors and drones are currently flying over fields and can "target the irrigation and the fertilization down to the individual plant," leading to productivity gains that are changing agriculture as we know it.[128]

So, we can do this in industries ranging from shoes to hairstyling to agriculture. But for some reason, the healthcare industry has yet to catch on. Why don't we have a similar app or model for our own health?

There's an old saying: "When all you have is a hammer, everything starts to look like a nail." That's how we practice medicine today, yet a treatment that works for one person may not work for another. That's because, just like your fingerprint is unique, there are other unique things about you, like your DNA. *Precision medicine*—healthcare customized for each unique individual—is the future.

---

128 https://www.bloomberg.com/news/videos/2018-03-14/bloomberg-presents-the-david-rubenstein-show-peer-to-peer-conversations-benjamin-netanyahu-video

PRECISION MEDICINE

Precision medicine will advance scientific discovery and improve clinical care. It will take into account each person's genes, environment, microbiome, and lifestyle, and tailor a unique treatment using sensors and electronic health record data. Think about our nutrition conversation. The recommended dietary allowance is based on a 2,000- to 2,500-calorie diet. But Olympic swimmer Michael Phelps packs away 10,000 calories a day.[129] So, if he were to consume the average amount of calories, he might never win a race. The law of averages is helpful, but it is also dangerous because it can lead us to a false sense of security. Imagine a drug of which half the population requires one milligram and the other half requires four milligrams. If you gave everyone 2.5 milligrams, you would underdose half of the population and overdose the other half.

Take high cholesterol, for example. Plavix may be the most commonly prescribed statin medication to prevent heart attacks and stroke, but it doesn't work for everyone. Currently, most people go through what's called step therapy, where you try one drug, and if that doesn't work for you, you try a different one, and so on. That process can take months and, in the meantime, you're not getting the medicinal impact of the right drug and may well be uncomfortable or even miserable. All that would be avoid-

129 https://www.menshealth.com/nutrition/michael-phelps-12000-calorie-diet-not-real

able with a simple $150 genetic test that can be done when you enroll in a health plan. By the time you show up, the doctor already has specific information on you, including which drugs are more likely to work for you and which are not. The old best practices in healthcare were reactive, but the new ones will be proactive, and data—your data—will be the foundation for those decisions.

Antibiotics indiscriminately kill bacteria in your body, but as I've mentioned, there is a lot of good bacteria in your body that should be left alone, or even encouraged and nourished. If antibiotics kill off certain strains of beneficial bacteria, doctors sometimes have to repopulate the body with those bacteria through various methods. But what if we could target only the bacteria we wanted to eliminate while not affecting the good bacteria? About 75 percent of people report that they would be willing to have sensors in their home that would monitor and share their information in real time, thus creating a feedback loop that would help them get the right amount of what they need. Being able to focus more specifically on the uniqueness of each individual makes medicine more like a scalpel than a hacksaw.

UNNECESSARY AND PREVENTABLE

Angelina Jolie did something that took immense courage. Based upon her family history, she knew she had a health risk. She took advantage of current gene technology and confirmed that she did in fact carry the gene that may cause several types of cancer. According to *The New York Times*, upon finding out that she carried the BRCA1 gene that made her predisposed to breast, ovarian, and pancreatic cancer, she had a double mastectomy[130] and removal of her ovaries and fallopian tubes[131] to improve her odds of not getting the cancer. She did it for her children. She also served as a role model by going public with the entire situation. That's a huge, and very brave, step to take, and should serve as an example to us all of what it looks like to take action and put the odds in our favor to prevent disease. This may have saved her from further unnecessary suffering—and possibly saved her life. Sometimes our devotion to others gives us the strength—that we might not have on our own—to act in the face of fear.

In the future, gene-editing technology will allow us to proactively correct these genetic mutations and the associated misery. A new gene-editing technology named **C**lustered **R**egularly **I**nterspaced **S**hort **P**alindromic **R**epeats (CRISPR)/Cas9[132] enables us to modify genes the same way a computer software package allows me to

---

130 http://www.nytimes.com/2013/05/14/opinion/my-medical-choice.html?_r=0

131 https://www.nytimes.com/2015/03/24/opinion/angelina-jolie-pitt-diary-of-a-surgery.html

132 https://www.ft.com/content/d6a773a0-cece-11e7-947e-f1ea5435bcc7?utm_source=The+Medical+Futurist+Newsletter&utm_campaign=c9ff6f9a00-Newsletter+2018%2F02%2F27&utm_medium=email&utm_term=0_efd6a3cd08-c9ff6f9a00-420520813

write and edit this document. Think about the difference between Gutenberg's printing press, the IBM electric typewriter, and the current version of Microsoft Word. Literally the difference between curing cancer is changing an "A" to a "C" in the genetic code, the same way you correct a misspelled word. That is the evolution we are taking with gene-editing technology. But of course, you still need to take action, no matter how great the technology becomes.

Now consider this: after you have had a heart attack, one thing you're supposed to do is take baby aspirin daily, as it has an incredibly high rate of preventing further heart attacks. But for whatever reason, many men don't do this incredibly simple thing. Look at the difference between a person who won't take some grape-flavored chewable baby aspirin to save his life, and Angelina Jolie. Starting today, and moving into the future, we will need to become adept at dealing with noncompliant behavior. I suggest we celebrate and reward the top 10 percent who do comply and manage the bottom 10 percent who don't—whatever that may look like.

Consider lung cancer, which kills more people than colon cancer and prostate cancer combined. Detecting lung cancer in the early stages is difficult because of the lack of symptoms. By the time you get a symptom, it's often too late, because it has already reached advanced stages and is difficult to cure. That gap is very unfortunate. But in recent years, doctors have found a low-dose CT (LDCT)[133] test that can be used to screen for lung cancer in people at high risk of the disease.[134] The test can help find some of these cancers early, which can lower the risk of dying from this disease. But if your doctor doesn't suggest you get this test, you should be aware of it, and ask for it. As new possibilities evolve, it is more important than ever to educate yourself on your options.

Apple recently introduced a significant update to the Health app, allowing customers to see their medical records right on their iPhone.[135] The updated Health Records section within the Health app brings together hospitals, clinics, and the existing Health app to make it easy for consumers to see their available medical data from multiple providers whenever they choose. Johns Hopkins Medicine, Cedars-Sinai, Penn Medicine, and other participating hospitals and clinics are among the first to make this beta feature available to their patients.[136] This will allow future apps that can tell any patient with

133 https://www.cancer.org/cancer/lung-cancer/prevention-and-early-detection/early-detection. html

134 https://www.cancer.org/cancer/lung-cancer/prevention-and-early-detection/exams-and-tests.html

135 http://www.wbur.org/commonhealth/2018/01/26/ apple-health-care-data?utm_source=facebook. com&utm_medium=social&utm_campaign=npr&utm_term=nprnews&utm_content=20180128

136 Apple, "Apple Announces Effortless Solution Bringing Health Records to iPhone," Apple Newsroom, press release, January 24, 2018. https://www.apple.com/newsroom/2018/01/ apple-announces-effortless-solution-bringing-health-records-to-iPhone/

enough data on their iPhone what questions they should ask their doctor about their diagnosis.

VALUE-BASED MEDICINE

After World War II, the United States decided that rebuilding Europe and Japan would be in everybody's interest. Consequently, a staff officer named Edwards Deming became one of the forefathers of the total quality management movement. Deming was on General Macarthur's staff, where he consulted as a staff officer. He also worked with high-level Japanese officials on statistics and quality metrics throughout the remainder of the forties and fifties. His work ultimately allowed Japanese society to rise from ruins to become the number two economy in the world, second only to the US. It led Japan's automotive industry to compete successfully against the US by the late seventies, using the concept of total quality management, which consists of forward-thinking metrics of quality. For example, if a particular component was supposed to be one foot long but they were allowed to have an eighth of an inch of variance, the Japanese machines might only have a sixteenth of an inch variance, even though they were allowed to have an eighth. The higher accuracy resulted in fewer breakdowns. In one case, Ford had two versions of a transmission that were available, one made in Japan and one not. People started buying the Ford with the Japanese-made transmission because it was higher quality and lasted longer.

What they found was that consumers were making decisions based on quality. The corollary here is that as doctors become better, as they use technology and forward-thinking processes, and as patients have access to that information, patients are going to make rational decisions in the same way that people wanted the Ford with the Japanese-built transmission—they'll want the higher quality. They'll know which one will break and which one won't. In healthcare today, it's hard to see which doctor or plan is broken and which one isn't. And as people in the market make rational decisions, we'll gain these efficiencies. That's called value-based care.

My overall theme in this book is that people need to take control of their own health, not just in terms of nutrition, movement, and mindset, but also in becoming knowledgeable about the healthcare system—for example, picking the right doctor or group of doctors for you. The future will allow us to make value-based decisions on the quality of care we are purchasing and the overall satisfaction we are likely to experience when making that transaction. It's important to know about both the weak points of the system, which need to work more efficiently, and the bright spots, which may offer opportunities to the healthcare consumer. The future will provide us the information we need to make these value-based decisions.

TAKING CONTROL OF YOUR HEALTH

The American Heart Association and the American Cancer Society are doing incredible work. It is most appropriate that two of the greatest organizations are fighting against two of the leading causes of death. I am a big supporter of both organizations and hope you are too. I also believe there are some areas we can help that may not be on the top-ten list but certainly need to be eliminated as soon as possible.

Type 2 diabetes, slip and fall prevention, and perhaps most importantly, end-of-life issues are some of the highest payout targets as we say in the military. These are three of the most preventable situations. The individual has a high degree of control to make a difference, and with a little help, I think we can have a big impact. This is not only the chance to positively impact you, your family, and your friends, but the entire nation, both physically and fiscally.

Type 2 diabetes is a miserable disease that can result in blindness, amputation, kidney failure, and more. It is also a very expensive disease, costing about $300 billion annually and largely preventable. This is a true case of the old adage, "it takes a village to raise a child." Combining the coordinated care model and expanding it to include nutrition and motivation demonstrate proven results to combat type 2 diabetes. There will be advances in technology, biology, and pharmacology. Until then, we all need to work together to help them to find the strength to fight this terrible disease. Evidenced-based diabetes-management programs, such as the Medicare Diabetes Prevention Program, are leading the way.[137] Three-hundred billion dollars in saved diabetes-related healthcare costs would pay the interest on the national debt.

Falls are not an inevitable part of aging, and they are largely preventable. After someone falls and breaks a hip or loses mobility, they tend to go downhill. Fear of future falls causes them to stay home more, which leads to social isolation and decreased mobility. Lack of mobility makes you vulnerable to illnesses. When people don't walk well, when they're wobbly or their gait is off, that is often a leading indicator that a fall is likely to happen. Being proactive, strengthening your legs, and improving your balance can prevent a fall. Falls are avoidable and easy to identify, yet not much is done to prevent them. Aside from isolation and depression, the direct associated medical costs are $34 billion, and that does not consider the additional costs or accelerated mortality rate.[138] In the future, we can reinforce standards for balance, range of motion, and strength as part of the annual physical that would greatly reduce this problem. Evidence-based programs, such as the STEADI Program, would pay for

137 https://innovation.cms.gov/initiatives/medicare-diabetes-prevention-program/

138 https://www.ncoa.org/resources/
falls-prevention-programs-saving-lives-saving-money-infographic-3/

the entire Supplemental Nutrition Assistance Program (SNAP, aka food stamps) for the nation.

Perhaps most controversial of all are end-of-life issues. Politicians can't talk about it because their opponents will hold it against them. Insurance providers can't talk about it because they'll seem self-serving. And people don't want to talk about it, because it requires them to face their own mortality. But the truth is, most people want to live and die in the comfort of their own home and on their own terms. Today we spend approximately 25 percent of each healthcare dollar in the final year of life. I think this is money well spent if that is the person's wish. However, if the person and their family do not want repeat visits to the intensive care unit, or to be hooked up to a machine to provide life support, I suggest we respect their wishes. I believe the future requires everyone to make decisions about their advance directives and socializing them with their loved ones and caregivers. This will allow people to live—and die—on their own terms and avoid costly efforts that are counter to their wishes. This would also result in saving approximately $150 billion, and we could probably put that money to use elsewhere.[139]

139 https://www.kff.org/medicare/issue-brief/medicare-spending-at-the-end-of-life/

CHAPTER 10

STAKEHOLDERS WORKING TOGETHER PROMOTE EFFICIENCIES

NEED-TO-KNOW NUGGETS

- Accountability versus responsibility.
- Stakeholders unlock new value.

ACCOUNTABILITY VERSUS RESPONSIBILITY

In the military, there's a big difference between *accountability* and *responsibility*. The main difference is that accountability cannot be shared while responsibility can. Responsibility is inherent in accountability. If you're the commander, you are accountable for virtually everything.

You are answerable for your actions. You may have subject-matter experts in place to help you, and you may delegate authority to them, thus making them responsible. We cannot delegate accountability.

At Advocate Health Advisors, I look at leading and lagging indicators of success. Lagging indicators include the things we already know, such as the number of sales we make and the company financials, and certainly these are important things. Leading indicators, on the other hand, are those behaviors and clues that provide insight about how we're going to perform in the future. It's hard to figure out what's important to measure and which metric will accurately provide insight into what you want to accomplish. But once you do, it is important to hit those numbers.

In my business, we assign somebody to be *accountable* for a specific metric. Now, they may not be directly *responsible* for a lot of the activities that lead to the metric, but they are *accountable*. Some people do the selling, and some do other things, but the person assigned the metric is accountable to me on a monthly basis. Establishing such roles and responsibilities is, I think, essential to accomplishing results. Timing is also important. Looking at leading indicators gives you a better grip on managing the business, and it's important to look at your measurements on a monthly basis. After all, if I wait until the end of the year to see how I did, I've missed my chance to influence things. If I do it six months before the end of the year, then I only have six months to influence things. But if I do it every week, I may spend so much time focusing on what the number is that I never get anything done. Monthly or quarterly checks allow you time to course correct if needed.

Similarly, if you've got a chronic condition, I believe you need daily monitoring and a monthly checkup. I think we can leverage technology, telemedicine, and other things to make that feasible. And not everything needs to be looked at by the doctor. Physicians' assistants and other professionals can handle a lot of it. That's also why leveraging technology to do the mundane work is key to making humans more productive. Doctors can spend more time doing what the doctor is uniquely qualified to do. That is not only more efficient, it is more enjoyable.

On the healthcare battlefield, as an individual, you're *accountable*. Your doctor is *responsible* for helping you maintain or improve your health. Your health plan is *responsible* for delivering the agreed-upon benefits that you've contracted with them for. Your government is *responsible* for protecting you. Your agent is *responsible* for helping you pick a plan—the right plan. At the end of the day, with all those responsible experts helping you, you're still *accountable*.

You're accountable to yourself, and we're all accountable to each other.

STAKEHOLDERS

All five of the stakeholders I discuss in this book—the individual, healthcare providers, carriers of health plans, the government, and independent agents—must work better together if we're going to resolve many of the problems that plague the healthcare industry. Too often they're at odds, and that's unnecessary and wasteful.

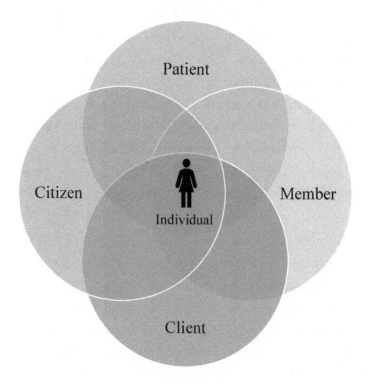

THE INDIVIDUAL

Many individuals are engaged in their own health, utilize their plans, and take an active role in their own healthcare. Of course, many more are not. Whether we use a carrot (incentives) or stick (penalties) approach, we should take action to influence otherwise inactive participants to become active.

If you smoke and are obese and have high blood pressure, should you pay the same premium as someone who doesn't? If you go to the gym and manage your health and eat right and make the hard choices and sacrifices it takes to live a healthy lifestyle, should you pay the same as people who don't? That doesn't seem fair. Alternatively, if you are born with the gene for a predisposition, that doesn't seem fair either. But this isn't about fairness, this is about taking control of your health and innovating to be the healthiest you possible.

People who become caregivers to friends and family and community members are true unsung heroes. Many are taking care of their parents and grandparents, for example. They house and feed them and help them make decisions. They're doing the right things for the right reasons and are working hard. These folks play a valuable role in our healthcare by filling the holes in the system and compensating for its inefficiencies. They should know that in most cases they can get help. They don't have to do it alone.

There are support groups, for example, that can connect them to resources and sources of information. As information becomes more transparent and more available from trusted sources, hopefully that will ease their burden a little and give them some tools they don't currently have.

Individuals will:

- Be responsible for their own wellbeing
- Be active participants in their own care
- Meet their obligation to care for friends, neighbors, and loved ones
- Stay informed—things are always changing
- Feel comfortable getting a second opinion
- Have access to advisory services the same way a librarian helps us find a book
- Have monitoring capabilities, sensors, and smartphones to help provide useful information
- Utilize nutrition, movement, and mindset as weapons to fight disease
- Understand that freedom isn't free—we have a civic responsibility

PROVIDERS

The doctor-patient relationship is sacred, and all the other stakeholders should be trying to enable, facilitate, and reinforce that relationship. Doctors and other healthcare providers are doing great things, working in the best interest of patients despite an inefficient system. Doctors are fighting that system and doing the best job they can with the resources they have. Sometimes it means they have to manipulate the system to do what's best for their patients.

The most successful medical-care teams I see today have cross-functional, multidisciplinary teams. They all work together and are organized around you, not the disease or their particular discipline. Doctors and other healthcare providers shouldn't be working in isolation.

When I was in Afghanistan as the operations officer, I had a team of various experts—people who were the best of the best in surveillance, medicine, intel, everything. When something happened, I could have the right person doing exactly what was needed within seconds. That only happened because all this expertise was coordinated under one system.

Providers will:

- Move toward personalized medicine and technology, giving them more time with the patient to focus on the human element of care
- Be more focused on customer service, as well as the value they provide
- Be organized and connected, and collaborate in real

time, face to face and virtually, with the entire health-care team, based on your unique care needs

CARRIERS/PAYERS

What carriers are doing well now is innovating. They're maximizing prevention and leveraging best practices. They also bring economic rationality to the practice of medicine, which is necessary because we don't have unlimited resources. We have to balance healthcare and economics, and carriers do that well. Private corporations, in this case the health-plan carriers, bring innovation because they have an incentive to bring down costs and promote choice.

Choice is good because you get what fits you best, and this leads to higher levels of customer satisfaction. If they can innovate and customers become more satisfied, and they can do this in an economically viable way, meeting all government requirements for outcomes and care and access, then that's a good thing. It's the best of both worlds because it plays to the strengths of each.

Among today's Medicare Advantage plans, most plans have value-added services or optional parts of the plan that focus on prevention. These include things like nutritional supplements, gym memberships, smoking-cessation programs, weight-loss programs, Jenny Craig, and so forth. We must emphasize the importance and value of these programs as people are selecting their plan. They can literally be life-changing and may offer thousands of dollars per year in additional benefits beyond what Original Medicare offers. These are called value-added items and services.

Medicare Advantage plans are good at focusing on prevention and treating chronic illnesses. You would think the government and the carrier would work together to encourage everybody to understand that. And you would think that, if they really keep people healthier and really drive costs down in the system, they would promote those successes.

Carriers will:

- Focus on prevention
- Focus on collaboration
- Innovate
- Bring efficiencies
- Bring economic perspective
- Promote choice and member satisfaction
- Evolve disease-state management

GOVERNMENT

The government has done many incredible things to

include the creation of the Medicare Advantage product and the Star Rating Systems. However, they do tend to make a new rule every time there's a problem. In particular with the Medicare and Medicaid services, every time someone misbehaves, the government makes a new rule to solve the problem. You shouldn't just "one to six it," a total quality management term for skipping the steps in decision making. What we need to do is define the inputs and the outputs.

All the stakeholders must work together to unlock new value—and the government has the lead role here. As much as people may understand that government is inefficient, they also know what the government does well, which is protect us. Our military is the best military in the world, perhaps in the history of the world. Ultimately, the president is the commander in chief of the military. Likewise, the healthcare system could run as efficiently as the military, given the right circumstances.

We can't just take it for granted, either, that the US as it's been will just continue forever. We as citizens need to take a role, we need to be active because this is high stakes. Its consequences reach beyond just us. The healthcare industry is so huge, its inefficiencies affect our entire economy. We're talking about a three-trillion-dollar healthcare system with potentially one trillion in waste. That's on top of the unnecessary loss of life and misery. Fixing healthcare can make the whole nation stronger. All levels of government play a key role here. All the different stakeholders add value, and working together with the individual's best interest at heart is how we can do the most good. No one entity or person can do it alone. Don't forget, the people who are most vulnerable, are least able to help themselves, and consume the most resources, often remain disenfranchised by the government who serves them. Ironically, the well-intended rules we make might be doing more harm than good.

Once, when I was in the military, I made a rule to solve a problem that led to controversy. We eventually concluded it was best to punish the individual and not the group. I do understand the tendency, when something bad happens, to ensure that it doesn't happen again—by making a new rule. That's human nature. But eventually we can make so many rules that they're all impossible to follow, and we'd be better off had we just done a better job of following the existing rules. We don't want the government (or anyone else) just blindly making blanket rules without understanding the nuances. I would like fewer rules and deeper wisdom. As Einstein said, "Furious activity is no substitute for understanding."

The federal government will:

- Continue to foster innovation and new technology
- Mine the data and provide metrics on how the providers are doing—allowing you to be better able to shop
- Continue to allow the individual to own their own medical records[140]
- Facilitate communication among the stakeholders to include privacy and security standards
- Align incentives and pay for performance
- Enable consumers to shop for care based on value— value-based medicine
- Offer awareness campaigns like they currently have for encouraging people to quit smoking[141]
- Remove rules that restrict access to care, services, and information
- Level the playing field for all Medicare programs. The rules around marketing plans, paying physicians, and hospital admissions vary by Medicare options.

State governments will:

- Work together to allow telemedicine and doctors to practice across state lines
- Work to find balance in the litigation rules
- Continue to work and support the underserved

Local governments will:

---

140 https://www.ncbi.nlm.nih.gov/pmc/articles/PMC1550638/

141 Smokefree.gov

- Provide real community interaction with those who need help and better matching of resources to needs
- Offer advisors available to help people make decisions, the same way the local librarian can help you find a book
- Coordinate with the providers to proactively designate high-risk individuals
- Orchestrate community-based (faith-based, service-based, non-profit) organizations in their support of healthy living and wellness
- Focus on preventing slips and falls (STEADI Program)[142]
- Encourage citizens to create and share advance directives
- Provide community-based type 2 diabetes prevention and self-management programs

AGENTS

Independent health-insurance agents do a good job of advising and helping people pick the plan that's in their best interest and making sure they're using that plan properly. I believe the agent of the future will serve as an extension of an individual healthcare team. I think they'll move up the value chain. For one thing, they're in the home, in many cases, and in a position to help enroll the client in the mail-order pharmacy to improve medication compliance, determine if the client qualifies for a Special

---

142 https://www.cdc.gov/STEADI/

Needs Plan, coordinate the in-home health and wellness assessment offered by carriers, and even socialize an approved falls-prevention checklist.

Ultimately, the agent should represent you, not the health plan, and just as individuals should be able to shop for a doctor, they should also be able to shop for an agent. We discussed that selecting the right team of doctors can literally help you live longer and better. These are very important, time-sensitive, and complicated decisions. These choices may have positive or negative consequences. You want a knowledgeable agent in your community who knows and understands the landscape to represent you.

Agents will:

- Genuinely care about their clients
- Help clients pick a plan, the right plan for them, and use that plan properly
- Assist the care team in assessing the social determinants of health for their client and getting them into the system for their initial wellness visit
- Maximize their in-home presence with the client
- Maximize their relationship with the client—the average agent spends several hours a year with their client and can be a positive influence
- Evolve into an advisory role and help clients connect with resources, services, and benefits

1980S TOTAL QUALITY MANAGEMENT PROCESS: AN EXAMPLE FOR HEALTHCARE TODAY

When I worked at IBM, there was a knowledge-management consultant named Lawrence Prusak. He said that you could not change a culture, but that you could change a process, and that process change could, in fact, lead to a cultural change. The following diagram is the process taken from my notes that we used when I first learned about total quality management. The former COO of Federal Express, James (Jim) Barksdale, was hired to run McCaw Cellular, which ultimately became the AT&T Wireless you know today. This worked well for those organizations.

1. **Identify improvement opportunities.** Here, we decide on which measures to focus on, opportunities for prevention of disease, and how to reduce costs. We listen to customers (individuals, patients, members, citizens, and clients) to find out what they like and don't like, what works and what doesn't. Then, we set priorities based on these opportunities. For example, many patients find it an irritating waste of time to have to fill out their entire medical history on a clipboard over and over every time they go to anybody for care. People also hate to have to wait. At Elite Health, the doctor enters the room at the same time you do, and

your electronic medical records are displayed on a wall in front of you in a private room on a big-screen TV.

2. **Identify inputs and outputs.** All stakeholders—individuals, providers, health plans, governments, and agents—must identify key customers and suppliers. I use those business terms, customers and suppliers, on purpose. Stakeholders must ask: who gets my output, and whose input do I need? Each stakeholder has a role here and can gain efficiency by defining the outputs and the inputs. That's where new value comes from. They say good, fast, or cheap—pick any two. We can make faster and better decisions, for example. In this case, we might be able to do all three because the system is so inefficient.

3. **Establish agreed-upon requirements.** What do you need from me and how do you need it? What do I give you and how do you want it? We must answer these questions. From there we can establish performance measures so that, under certain circumstances, we should be able to perform at a particular level. For example, if Katie's cancer center needed to know specific details about the melanoma cancer she has, the pathology center that reported the presence of cancer should do so in a level of detail that would allow the cancer center to select the appropriate course of action without lengthy delays. The agreed-upon requirement here is that it is not enough to say she has melanoma.

We need to know the exact type of melanoma, so the exact treatment can be prescribed.

4. **Identify gaps.** On the basis of your data, we identify the gaps between what customers need and what your work process can supply. There are plenty of these to choose from, and I've called out several in this book. There is a need for serious talk about end-of-life issues. There is a gap between how people want to live—and die—in their final days and how the system treats them. Gaps are everywhere, and we need to continue to identify and fix them.

5. **Describe and analyze the current process.** This may involve flow charting, looking at bottlenecks, and engaging in root-cause analysis of breakdowns and why they happen. Does the current process consistently meet customer requirements or not? Think about the hospital example: each of the departments in the hospital did a great job of admitting and providing the appropriate services in a timely manner. Yet, the overall customer wait time was eight hours because the departments operated independently, and the overall efforts were not coordinated. So, in isolation, the independent departments get high marks, but that does not reflect the overall customer experience.

6. **Develop and execute solutions.** This naturally follows when you find that the current process doesn't work. You fix it, so it does work. And if it still doesn't meet requirements, you may need to develop a new

process. Maybe you also have contingency diagrams and checklists to anticipate problems. Data and analytics are only making it easier and easier to fix problems. Execution becomes its own challenge, but that challenge means you're into the solution part of the process, which is good. But note that if the government or anybody else says, "here's the problem and here's the solution," it means they skipped all those other steps—they "one-to-sixed" it.

7. **Measure and monitor.** At this stage, we identify leading and lagging indicators of success, set benchmarks, create a feedback system, document the results, and make it all transparent so people can shop and know what the results are. Allowing the consumer to shop for value will fundamentally change the way the industry operates today, the same way consumers knew to buy the Ford with the better transmission. The government is making strides through publicly available Star Rating Systems, which measure and compare health plans, hospitals, and doctors, based on a standard set of measures.

OPERATION NEPTUNE'S SPEAR

On May 1, 2011, President Obama addressed the nation and announced that Osama bin Laden had been killed, calling it "the most significant achievement to date in our nation's effort to defeat al Qaeda."

The covert mission to kill Osama bin Laden, code-named Operation Neptune's Spear, was conducted by the Army, Navy, and Air Force. This time, the Navy was in the lead, specifically the Navy SEALs. In contrast to Operation Eagle Claw in the eighties, the different military units used in this operation knew and communicated with each other. The services trained together and even had a life-sized replica of the compound. There was a clearly established chain of command and a command post on scene.

The White House leadership watched in real time as helicopters entered the compound, searched the area, and hit the jackpot. Shortly after, not only the White House, but the entire world, learned of the successful operation. The multifunctional team that conducted this operation, including the CIA, had served together many times over a decade of war. They effectively "grew up" together.[143]

Operation Eagle Claw led to the creation of the US Special Operations Command, based on the findings of the Holloway Report. The USSOCOM created an even more elite unified organization that conducted Operation Neptune's Spear. The mission's success epitomizes a victory from lessons learned some thirty years prior.

What will our healthcare victories be? What is the healthcare equivalent of the US Special Operations Command?

---

143 https://www.newyorker.com/magazine/2011/08/08/getting-bin-laden

How will our stakeholders work together in the new coordinated environment?

CONCLUSION

The time to arm yourself is now.

We've conducted the mission analysis. We've identified courses of action. The combat orders have been issued.

WE ARE AT WAR AND YOU'RE ON THE BATTLEFIELD

The war is happening. Lives are being lost, and trillions of dollars are being wasted on an antiquated system that can cure or kill you—and whether you like it or not, you're on that battlefield. So are your loved ones. We all are.

Again, this is literally an issue of national security. Because the healthcare industry is so large, it represents a significant amount of our economy that actually *exceeds* the cost of war, both in the number of lives lost and dollars spent. Subsequently, the decisions we make matter, and we have an obligation as citizens, parents, and children to take an active role in our own well-being. Ultimately, if you are stronger, the nation is stronger.

We've identified the leading causes of death. Go ahead and look at them again. But remember, when you look beyond those major causes of death, what you usually find are smoking, obesity, a sedentary lifestyle, and negative feelings. If we all start taking better care of ourselves, we're beating death in most of the ways it finds us.

Two other causes of death that we can't overlook are medical errors and noncompliant behavior. Remember, it's the system and your attitude toward the system that cause a lot of the harm. More than 250,000 people die each year because of our fragmented system of healthcare, and probably even more die because they didn't do what their doctor told them, for example, to take their medicine. That system needs to change, but it is still the battlefield we must fight on today. It's our responsibility to understand it, navigate it, and help our brothers and sisters in arms do the same.

While we must deal with the current system, we must all expect more. We should demand the same level of value, efficiency, and customer service that we see in other industries. We can apply military lessons learned. Just as the military grew stronger out of the ashes of Operation Eagle Claw, so too can our own system rise to new heights.

YOUR JOB

Part II of the book diverts the reader to what is immediately available to actively arm themselves for the battle at hand. There is no dependency on law, politics, or technology. The arsenals of nutrition, movement, and mindset are immediately available to the active healthcare participant.

Remember, it doesn't even matter if you, or your loved ones, are not sick or unhealthy right now. This is about preparation. It's about building your hill or, if you're over that hill, managing it. How comfortable are you talking with your primary-care physician? Are you ready for what could happen? What are you eating? Are you exercising? What are your vulnerabilities? Are you really properly armed?

You know your weapons. Nutrition. Movement. Mindset. You've been trained. Now, it's a matter of execution.

Nutrition is the single most important thing you can do to influence your health. Understanding that a lack of vitamins and minerals can make you sick is proof that the ideal amounts of vitamins and minerals can keep you well. You are, literally, what you eat. What you put in your body doesn't just become you, it communicates with the rest of your body, telling it what to do. You must send your body the right messages. The evolving fields of epigenetics and the microbiome reveal a new relationship between you, your environment, and the chemical instructions we receive with each bite of food we take.

But no matter how optimal your nutritional intake, if you do not move enough, you will never get those nutrients where they need to be, nor will you remove the toxins from where they do not belong. Your body is an advanced machine. We all understand that if you do not use a vehicle, it will eventually seize up. Similarly, just as your body was made to move, there is an ideal amount of activity, strength, flexibility, and conditioning for each of us. You create your own energy.

Perhaps most powerful, yet least understood, is the power of the human mind. The contrapositive tells us that, just as you can worry yourself sick, you can will yourself well. You can hack happiness. Resilience, happiness, and coping skills are things we can build and influence, no matter what our individual genetic predisposition. Remember, genes load the gun, but environment pulls the trigger. Your mindset is perhaps the biggest determinant of your environment because we have freewill and we live in a free country. Preparing your mind is just as important as preparing your body for the fight ahead.

WHAT'S WORKING NOW

Despite its being fragmented, there are parts of the system

that are working well, and there are exciting technologies on the horizon we should keep an eye on.

One of the best things working right now is the stability, dependability, backing, and oversight of the federal government combined with the choice, innovation, and high level of efficiency and customer satisfaction that only well-run private companies can offer. We see this manifested in the creation of Medicare Part C, also known as Medicare Advantage, where private companies can deliver the Original Medicare benefits and more. Perhaps best of all, we see the evolution of Special Needs Programs that directly protect those who need them most. Ironically, the government rules designed to protect those people actually serve as a barrier to getting them the resources they so desperately need. There are things working, but there's much farther to go.

New technologies are evolving and converging to change the world as we know it today. Some people think computers will become smarter than people in our lifetime. As promising as these technologies are, we must be vigilant to ensure that speedy adoption and democratization do not lag. Historically, it can take more than a decade for a proven medical innovation to matriculate through the system. As these technologies result in new treatment options, it's on us to be aware of how to access them.

Perhaps what is most exciting on the horizon is personalized medicine. Personalized medicine is the future, and with that personalization will come yet another round of exponential gains. The healthcare industry will finally catch up and perhaps surpass other industries—and it should, given the importance of what we are dealing with. Creating a virtual model of yourself to include your genome, microbiome, and environment will enable you to accurately predict the best prevention or cure for you. The evolution of these technologies and capabilities will make it even more important that you actively participate in your role as an accountable and responsible person, as a patient, member, citizen, and client in your own well-being and that of your friends and loved ones.

THE WORK AHEAD

As we all work together in our respective roles, let's not lose sight of the immediate opportunity to help each other today in the areas of type 2 diabetes, slip-and-fall prevention, and end-of-life issues. These gains will not only save lives and avoid misery, but they will yield a significant financial benefit to the nation. I know it sounds like a stretch, but the economic value we are talking about here of hundreds of billions of dollars (trillions, over time) literally can have a fiscal impact to the country that is so big it could actually impact national security. Remember, Secretary of Defense Mattis recently agreed that the biggest threat we have to our national security is the debt.

HEALTHCARE SOURCES OF WASTE VERSUS FEDERAL BUDGET EXPENDITURES

Healthcare Sources of Waste	Cost	Could Offset These Programs	Cost
Unnecessary Services	$210B	Federal Budget Deficit[144]	$228B
Excessive Administrative Costs	$190B	Interest on Debt[145]	$241B
Inefficient Delivered Services	$130B	Medicare Program[146]	$591B
Overpriced Services	$105B	Medicaid[147]	$385B
Fraud	$75B	Supplemental Nutrition Assistance Program a.k.a. Food Stamps[148]	$70B
Missed Prevention	$55B	DOD Budget[149]	$639B
Type 2 Diabetes	$300B		
Slips & Falls	$34B		
End of Life	$150B		
	$1.25T		$2.15T

Does not include the National Debt of $20T.

There is no organization where the concept of shared responsibility is better modeled than in the military. That's just part of the military culture. We hold each other accountable. We "police" one another. We have a saying: "If you walk by something not up to standard, then you set a new standard." I think we need to adopt this in our own culture, outside the military.

We should care about each other enough to police each other. Right now, it's not okay to say something to someone who's smoking, or who is obese, or is walking with a wobbly gait. How do we help each other to live

144 https://www.cbo.gov/publication/53443

145 https://www.cbo.gov/sites/default/files/115th-congress-2017-2018/graphic/52408-budgetoverall.pdf

146 https://www.cbo.gov/publication/53624

147 https://www.cbo.gov/topics/health-care

148 https://www.cbpp.org/research/policy-basics-introduction-to-the-supplemental-nutrition-assistance-program-snap

149 https://www.defense.gov/News/News-Releases/News-Release-View/Article/1190216/dod-releases-fiscal-year-2018-budget-proposal/

healthier lifestyles? Remember, this all adds up to something significant.

I believe those of us who have the knowledge and ability to help one another, have the obligation to do so. The ideal way to do this is through tightly knit groups, because they communicate better. Like-minded organizations share a common bond, the bond creates trust, and the trust empowers members to speak and listen to help each other. For example, my son and I were looking over a closed ski path when two passersby said, "Be careful; don't do that; you do not want to do that." We were complete strangers, but because we had poles and skies, they were comfortable being helpful, and I was appreciative. In contrast, I walk by smokers every day, and while I might think of saying, "Be careful; don't do that; you do not want to do that," it is inappropriate because it would not be well received. This is why we need to work through trusted relationships.

I am calling on all members of organizations that help others—particularly my fellow Veterans—to join me in declaring war against type 2 diabetes, slips and falls, and end-of-life issues. National initiatives exist today that provide turn-key, evidenced-based medicine programs. These are proven battle plans that will eradicate the enemies that prey on our communities. I believe this is the most efficient use of our time and energy, in terms of serving the greater good for individuals and, ultimately, our nation.

We need innovative ways to solve these problems. To get something different, we must do something differently. When I was in college, I saw the same homeless person holding a sign at the traffic light. It made me uncomfortable. I was torn between wanting to give them money and not supporting bad habits that may have gotten them there in the first place. I tried to do some volunteer work and eventually raised money for charity, but it did not ease my discomfort when I returned to that stoplight where I tried to avoid eye contact. Then I got an idea.

It was simple. I got the information of the nearest shelter where they could get food and help. I also bought a case of beer. I taped the cards with the information on the top of the beer cans so they would need to remove it before drinking the beer. It was a compromise, but it worked for me.

Let's remember this all comes down to individuals taking an active role in their own health, in addition to helping others.

THE POWER IS OURS

The American healthcare system is vast and complex.

But for all its many shortcomings and inefficiencies, it also offers opportunity as society, technology, and public policy are converging to finally address the current needs of the population. The system is, in fact, going to change, and that is an exciting thing.

Life offers no promise except an ending. Facing our own mortality is a necessity, uncomfortable as it may seem at first. It helps us find our priorities. For most people, that turns out to be living and dying on our own terms. Living life on our own terms is how you win the fight on the healthcare battlefield. It also lets you find comfort in the days that you have left.

We can take charge of our health and navigate the healthcare system—or we can become like a pinball in a pinball machine and let the system bang us around until we drop out of sight. This is our choice, but having a choice, even a hard choice, is a gift. Human beings are the only animals that have a choice between a stimulus and a response. Healthcare choices are hard. Choosing a healthy lifestyle, summoning self-discipline, educating yourself, facing your fears—these are all hard. The fact is that a lot of things in our lives are hard, but the alternatives are even harder. We need to rise to the occasion, and I believe we will.

I know things about my family and friends because they're people that I care about. I know little things. I know my wife likes cream with her coffee, and I know that my friend Wayne likes Splenda and cream with his coffee. I know these details and take interest in them because I care about these people. Likewise, if you care about yourself, which you should, you should take at least that much interest in yourself. You should know about your health because it matters. Health is precious.

There will be a battle. Lives will be won or lost based on the decisions you make and the actions you take. You have the opportunity to save not only your life, but the lives of those around you.

My goals in this book have been to inform and enlighten people, to start a dialogue, to encourage awareness, and to inspire taking action and control of your own well-being. If there's one takeaway here, it's that you have the power to take charge of your own health and navigate your family to safety. Eat right, be active, and improve your mindset because, in the end, you're accountable for your choices.

We have a choice every day. We can wake up, and we can be happy—or not.

In a commencement speech that ended up going viral, Admiral McRaven, my former boss, told us things you can learn from a Navy SEAL. You'd think a man of his experience and rank would talk about things we'd never heard of before, but what he talked about was one of the simplest things you could think of, something that—like our own health—was as important as it was easy to overlook.

Here's what he said:

> Every morning in basic SEAL training, my instructors, who at the time were all Vietnam veterans, would show up in my barracks room, and the first thing they would inspect was your bed. If you did it right, the corners would be square, the covers pulled tight, the pillow centered just under the headboard and the extra blanket folded neatly at the foot of the rack—that's Navy talk for bed.
>
> It was a simple task—mundane at best. But every morning we were required to make our bed to perfection. It seemed a little ridiculous at the time, particularly in light of the fact that we were aspiring to be real warriors, tough battle-hardened SEALs, but the wisdom of this simple act has been proven to me many times over.
>
> If you make your bed every morning, you will have accomplished the first task of the day. It will give you a small sense of pride, and it will encourage you to do another task and another and another. By the end of the day, that one task completed will have turned into many tasks completed. Making your bed will also

reinforce the fact that little things in life matter. If you can't do the little things right, you will never do the big things right.

And if, by chance, you have a miserable day, you will come home to a bed that is made—that you made—and a made bed gives you encouragement that tomorrow will be better.

It starts with the simplest things, things which I've laid out in this book. Taking the easy steps to look after your own health can lead to us taking further action and helping each other. And if, at the end of a tough day, we haven't helped as many people as we'd wished, we can at least rest easy in the equivalent of our own made bed—our healthier, stronger bodies and minds that, in turn, are making our nation stronger.

ABOUT THE AUTHOR

DARWIN HALE is the CEO of Advocate Health Advisors, a company he founded to help people make the best decisions about their healthcare. A decorated officer, Hale served over thirty years in the military, ranging from peacekeeping operations to combat with US Special Operations Command in support of the Global War on Terror. Concurrently, in the world of business, he worked with some of the top companies in the fields of healthcare services, information technologies, telecommunications, and personnel management. *Need to Know* reflects a lifetime of learning what works (and what doesn't) inside some of the most successful organizations in the world.